THE

CHARTER AND ORDINANCES

OF THE

CITY OF BATTLE CREEK.

Published by Authority of the Common Council.

BATTLE CREEK.
STEAM PRESS OF THE REVIEW AND HERALD OFFICE.
1861.

PRESENTED TO

THE ENGLISH LIBRARY

OF THE

UNIVERSITY OF MICHIGAN

BY

Mrs. John Sheffield
of Battle Creek

THE

CHARTER AND ORDINANCES

OF THE

CITY OF BATTLE CREEK.

Published by Authority of the Common Council.

BATTLE CREEK.
STEAM PRESS OF THE REVIEW AND HERALD OFFICE.
1861.

Resolution of the Common Council.

Resolved, That the Committee on Printing is hereby authorized and directed to cause to be published in a book, copies of the CHARTER and ORDINANCES of the City of Battle Creek, together with the Rules of Business, and such other matters as may seem proper, and that the Committee be authorized to contract for said work in the name of the City.

CHESTER BUCKLEY,
ERASTUS HUSSEY,
EDWARD COX.
Committee on Printing.

Rules of Business.

The business of all regular meetings of the Common Council, after reading the minutes of the preceding meeting, shall be as follows:

1. Presentation and referring Petitions.
2. Reports of Standing Committees.
3. " " Special "
4. " " City Attorney.
5. " " Chief Engineer.
6. " " Marshal.
7. " " Street Commissioner.
8. " " Treasurer.
9. " " Fire Wardens.
10. Motions and Resolutions.
11. Unfinished Business.
12. Special Orders.

ALDERMEN.

1859	LEONIDAS D. DIBBLE, F. M. SANDERSON.	*First Ward.*
1859	EDWARD COX, SAMUEL S. STEWART.	*Second Ward.*
1859	ERASTUS HUSSEY, CHARLES MASON.	*Third Ward.*
1859	VICTORY P. COLLIER, WILLIAM H. SKINNER.	*Fourth Ward*
1860	F. M. SANDERSON, LEONIDAS D. DIBBLE.	*First Ward.*
1860	L. ETHERIDGE, EDWARD COX.	*Second Ward.*
1860	CHESTER BUCKLEY, ERASTUS HUSSEY.	*Third Ward.*
1860	BENJAMIN F. HINMAN VICTORY P. COLLIER.	*Fourth Ward.*
1861	F. M. SANDERSON, HENRY CANTINE.	*First Ward.*
1861	EDWARD COX, L. ETHERIDGE.	*Second Ward.*
1861	ERASTUS HUSSEY, CHESTER BUCKLEY.	*Third Ward.*
1861	VICTORY P. COLLIER, B. F. HINMAN.	*Fourth Ward.*

OFFICERS

OF THE CITY OF BATTLE CREEK.

Organized February 25th, 1859.

MAYORS.

		Votes Polled.
1859	ELIJAH W. PENDILL	699
1860	ELIJAH W. PENDILL	753
1861	ELIJAH W. PENDILL.*	734
1861	CHARLES S. GRAY.	Appointed Nov. 11, 1861.

RECORDERS.

1859 WILLIAM F. NEALE. 1860 WILLIAM F. NEALE.

1861 PAUL GEDDES.

MARSHALS.

1859 MOSES B. RUSSELL. 1860 JAMES B. MASON.

1861 JAMES B. MASON,† 1861 SILAS G. PETTEE,‡

ATTORNEYS.

1859 MYRON H. JOY. 1860 LEONARD H. STEWART.

1861 LEVANT C. RHINES. 1861 LEONIDAS D. DIBBLE.

---

*Resigned Nov. 4, 1861. †Resigned. ‡Appointed.

OFFICERS

OF THE VILLAGE OF BATTLE CREEK.

Organized A. D. 1850.

Presidents.

A. D.		VOTES POLLED.
1850	William Brooks.	241
1851	Charles Mason.	146
1852	Charles Mason.	146
1853	Edward Cox.	256
1854	Roswell T. Merrill.	329
1855	Roswell T. Merrill.	315
1856	Chester Buckley.	483
1857	Chester Buckley.	475
1858	Jonathan Hart.*	635
1858	Leander Etheridge, (to fill vacancy.)	Appointed.

Marshals.

1850	Franklin S. Clarke.
1851	George C. Rogers.
1852	Joseph Babcock.
1853	Silas Cox.*
1854	James W. Brown.
1855	John Caldwell.
1856	John Caldwell.
1857	John Caldwell.
1858	Joseph Babcock.

Clerks.

1850	Isaac C. Mott.
1851	Dwight May.
1852	Leonard H. Stewart.
1853	Leonard H. Stewart.
1854	Charles S. May, (Resigned July 13, 1854.)
1854	Eli L. Stillson, (Appointed to fill vacancy.)
1855	Joseph Dodge.
1856	William F. Neale.
1857	Cornelius Byington.
1858	William F. Neale.

*Deceased.

CITY CHARTER.

AN ACT TO INCORPORATE

THE

CITY OF BATTLE CREEK.

SECTION 1. *The People of the State of Michigan enact,* That sections one and twelve of the township of Battle Creek, and sections six and seven of the township of Emmett, in the county of Calhoun, be and the same are hereby set off from the townships of Battle Creek and Emmett respectively, and declared to be a city by the name of the "City of Battle Creek," by which name it shall be hereafter known. Boundaries. Name.

SEC. 2. The inhabitants of said city, from time to time, shall be and continue a body corporate and politic, to be known and distinguished by the name and title of the mayor, recorder and aldermen of the city of Battle Creek, and shall be and are hereby made capable of suing and being sued, of pleading and being impleaded, of answering and being answered unto, and of defending and being defended in all courts of law and equity, and in all other places whatever; and may have a common seal, which they may alter and change at pleasure, and by the same name shall be and are hereby made capable of purchasing, holding, conveying and disposing of any real and personal estate for said city. Corporate name and powers.

SEC. 3. The said city shall be divided into four wards as follows, to wit: The first ward shall embrace all that portion of the city described as follows: beginning at the point where the Battle Creek intersects the east line of section six of township two south of range seven west, thence southerly on the east lines of sections six and seven of said township, to the south-east corner of said section seven; thence westerly on the south line of said section seven to the south-west corner thereof; thence northerly on the west line of said section seven to the south-east Wards. First.

AN ACT TO INCORPORATE
THE
CITY OF BATTLE CREEK.

SECTION 1. *The People of the State of Michigan enact*, That sections one and twelve of the township of Battle Creek, and sections six and seven of the township of Emmett, in the county of Calhoun, be and the same are hereby set off from the townships of Battle Creek and Emmett respectively, and declared to be a city by the name of the "City of Battle Creek," by which name it shall be hereafter known. Boundaries. Name.

SEC. 2. The inhabitants of said city, from time to time, shall be and continue a body corporate and politic, to be known and distinguished by the name and title of the mayor, recorder and aldermen of the city of Battle Creek, and shall be and are hereby made capable of suing and being sued, of pleading and being impleaded, of answering and being answered unto, and of defending and being defended in all courts of law and equity, and in all other places whatever; and may have a common seal, which they may alter and change at pleasure, and by the same name shall be and are hereby made capable of purchasing, holding, conveying and disposing of any real and personal estate for said city. Corporate name and powers.

SEC. 3. The said city shall be divided into four wards as follows, to wit: The first ward shall embrace all that portion of the city described as follows: beginning at the point where the Battle Creek intersects the east line of section six of township two south of range seven west, thence southerly on the east lines of sections six and seven of said township, to the south-east corner of said section seven; thence westerly on the south line of said section seven to the south-west corner thereof; thence northerly on the west line of said section seven to the south-east Wards. First.

corner of section twelve in township two south, of range eight west; thence westerly on the south line of said section twelve to the south-west corner thereof; thence northerly on the west line of said section twelve, to the center of Race street, as laid down on Meachem's Addition to Battle Creek; thence along the center of Race street to the intersection of Race and Jefferson streets; thence northerly along the center of Jefferson street to the intersection of Jefferson street and the Battle Creek; thence up along the center of the Battle Creek to the place of beginning.

Second. The second ward shall embrace all that portion of the city described as follows: beginning at the intersection of Jefferson street and the Battle Creek, thence southwesterly along the center of Jefferson street to the intersection of Jefferson and Race streets; thence along the center of Race street to the west line of said section twelve; thence northerly along the west line of said section twelve, and the west line of section six in the township last named, to the intersection of Main street with said last named section line; thence south-easterly along the center of Main street to the intersection of said street and Battle Creek; thence up along the center of said Battle Creek to the place of beginning.

Third. The third ward shall embrace all that portion of the city described as follows: beginning at the intersection of the Battle Creek and the west line of said section seven; thence down along the center of the Battle Creek to the intersection of the Battle Creek and Main street; thence north-westerly along the center of Main street to its intersection with the west line of section one in township two south, of range eight west aforesaid; thence northerly along the west line of said section one to the north-west corner thereof; then easterly along the north line of said section one to the north-east corner thereof; thence southerly along the east line of said township two south, of range eight west, to the place of beginning.

Fourth. The fourth ward shall embrace all that portion of the city described as follows: all of those parts of said sections six and seven in township two south, of range seven west, lying north of the Battle Creek: *Provided*,

That whenever a street or water-course is mentioned in this act as a boundary or division line, the center of said street or water-course shall be deemed to be the said line or boundary. Proviso.

Sec. 4. The following officers shall be elected from among the electors of said city, to wit: one mayor, one recorder, who shall be ex-officio school inspector and city clerk, one supervisor, one treasurer, one marshal, who shall be ex-officio street-commissioner, two school inspectors, two directors of the poor, and four justices of the peace, who shall be elected in the following manner, to wit: the mayor, recorder, supervisor, treasurer and marshal shall be elected annually, and shall hold their offices for one year and until their successors shall be elected and qualified. There shall also be elected, annually, one school inspector and one director of the poor, who shall hold their offices for two years and until their successors shall be elected and qualified: *Provided*, That at the first election held under this act, two school inspectors and two directors of the poor shall be elected, and that immediately after said first election the common council shall meet and determine by lot which of the school inspectors and which of the directors of the poor, shall hold for one year and which for two years. There shall also be elected, annually, one justice of the peace, who shall hold his office for four years and until his successor shall be elected and qualified: *Provided*, That at the first election under this act, four justices of the peace shall be elected, who shall be justices of the peace of said city, one of whom shall hold his office during the term of one year, one for the term of two years, one for the term of three years, and one for the full term of four years, and until their successors shall be elected and qualified; and that the term for which said justices are elected at said first election shall be designated on the ballots. Officers. Terms of office. Certain officers to be classified. Justices of the peace. Proviso. Term of office.

Sec. 5. There shall be elected at the same time in the several wards from among the electors thereof respectively, one alderman and one constable; the said alderman to hold his office for two years, and the said constable for one Ward officers.

year, and until their successors shall be elected and qualified: *Provided*, That at the first election under this act two aldermen shall be elected in each ward, one for the term of one year, and one for the full term of two years, and until their successors shall be elected and qualified; and that the term for which said aldermen are elected at said first election shall be designated on the ballots.

Proviso. Terms.

Annual elections. SEC. 6. The annual election under this act shall be held on the first Monday of March in each year, at such place in each of the several wards as the common council shall designate, notice of which shall be given by the recorder at least eight days before the election, by posting printed notices thereof in three public places in each ward; the aldermen of each ward and an elector residing in said ward, who shall be appointed by the common council at the regular meeting thereof next preceding said election, shall be the inspectors of such election; and they shall also be inspectors of all elections to be held in said city. The said inspectors shall, before opening the polls at any election, appoint one of their own number chairman of such board of inspectors, they shall also appoint some person who shall be an elector of said ward to act as clerk of said election: *Provided*, That at the general and judicial elections they shall appoint two such clerks. In case of the absence of one or more of such inspectors, the electors present may choose *viva voce* from their number, one or more to fill such vacancy or vacancies, to whom and to such clerk or clerks, and to the inspectors so appointed by the common council, shall be administered the constitutional oath by either of said aldermen, or by any justice of the peace of said city. The manner of conducting all elections, and canvassing the votes and the qualifications of electors in the several wards, shall be the same as in townships; the word "ward" instead of "township" being used in the oath to be administered to an elector in case his vote shall be challenged, and also in the making of all certificates or statements of and concerning such elections: *Provided*, That at such charter election the said ward inspectors shall make one certificate of the num-

Notice. Who to be inspectors. Their duties. Proviso. Vacancies. Oath. Manner of conducting elections. Certificates of votes given.

ber of votes given for each person for the several offices to be filled in the said city, and also one certificate of the officers elected in and for their respective wards, which certificates shall be within twenty-four hours filed in the office of the recorder of said city; and upon the Thursday next following the day of such election, the common council shall meet at the office of the said recorder and thereupon determine who, by the greatest number of votes given in the several wards, are duly elected to fill the respective city offices; and it shall be the duty of the said recorder, immediately after such determination, to cause notice to be given to each of the persons elected of their election. And each of said officers so elected and notified shall, within five days thereafter, take and subscribe the constitutional oath of office before any person authorized to administer oaths, and shall deliver the same to the said recorder, who shall file the same in his office: *Provided*, That in case of the election of one or more justices of the peace, and of the election and qualification of one or more constables, the said recorder shall make a certificate thereof, and cause it to be delivered to the clerk of the said county of Calhoun, in the same manner as is required of township clerks: *Provided also*, That all justices of the peace and constables elected under this act shall, within five days after receiving notice of their election, qualify by filing their constitutional oath, and giving security in the same manner as required by law of justices of the peace and constables of townships; and in case two or more persons shall receive for the same city office an equal number, and a plurality of the votes given at such election, the common council shall immediately proceed to determine by lot between the persons so receiving the highest number of votes, which shall be considered elected to such city office; and in case two or more persons shall receive for the same ward office, an equal number and a plurality of the votes given at such election, the said board of ward inspectors shall, immediately after such election, proceed to determine by lot between the persons so receiving the highest number of votes, which shall be considered

Common council to canvass for city officer

Notice.

Oath of office.

Proviso.

Justices to file oath.

In case of tie the election determined by lot.

elected to such office; and in case any of the officers so elected and notified shall neglect for the term of five days to qualify as aforesaid, or to give such security as the provisions of this act, or the by-laws or ordinances of the common council of said city shall require, such officer or officers shall be deemed to have declined.

Common council to appoint certain officers.

SEC. 7. The common council shall have power to appoint an attorney for the city, one or more deputy street commissioners, and such other officers, whose election is not herein specifically provided for, as they may deem necessary to carry into effect the powers granted by this act, and to remove the same at pleasure.

Vacancies, how filled.

And in case of the death, resignation, or neglect to qualify, or removal from the city, or from the ward for which he was elected, of any officer of the corporation, the common council shall, as soon as may be, appoint an officer to fill such vacancy, to hold and serve until such vacancy shall be filled by an election for the unexpired portion of the term of said office; and all officers so appointed shall be notified and qualified as herein directed:

Proviso.

Provided, That the common council shall, in case any vacancy shall occur, forthwith order a special election to fill vacancies in any office which is elective under this act;

Vacancies in elective offices, how filled.

in which case the common council shall designate the time and place for holding such special election, and the same notice shall be given as for an annual election, stating the office or offices to be filled; and any person so elected shall hold and serve for the remainder of the term of such office.

Duties of village officers relative to first election.

SEC. 8. The president, clerk and trustees of the village of Battle Creek shall have all the powers, and are hereby required to discharge all the duties in relation to the first election to be held under this act, that are conferred upon the aldermen and inspectors in each ward of the city of Battle Creek, any two of whom may act as inspectors of election in either of the wards at such election. And in case no two of them shall appear at the time and place appointed for such election, one or more persons shall be chosen from the electors present to act as inspectors;

Notice.

notice of which first election shall be given by the clerk of said village in the same manner as is required of the recorder of said city.

Recorder to act in absence of mayor.

SEC. 9. In case of the absence or sickness of the mayor, or of a vacancy occurring in said office, the recorder shall be and he is hereby authorized to do and perform all the duties and trusts appertaining to the said office of mayor (except to preside at meetings of the common council), until the said mayor resume his duties, or another be elected and qualified.

Who to constitute common council.

SEC. 10. The mayor, recorder, and aldermen, when assembled together and duly organized, shall constitute the common council of the city of Battle Creek, and a majority of the whole shall be necessary to constitute a quorum for the transaction of business, though a less number may adjourn the council from time to time; and said common council shall meet at such times as they shall determine, and at such other times as the mayor, or in case of his sickness or absence, the recorder may appoint; and the said common council shall have power to impose, levy and collect such fines as they may deem proper for the non-attendance of the members and officers thereof, at such meeting, and also to require the attendance at such meetings of any officer of said city, and to impose fines for non-attendance. It shall be the duty of the mayor to preside at all meetings of the common council, and in case of a tie, to give the casting vote. And it shall, also, be the duty of the recorder to attend all such meetings, and keep a fair and accurate report of their proceedings, which shall be published in one or more papers published in said city. In case the mayor shall be absent, the common council may appoint one of their number to preside at such meeting; and in case of the absence of the recorder, they may appoint one of their own number a recorder *pro tempore*.

Quorum.

Meetings.

Fines for non-attendance.

Duties of mayor.

Recorder.

Certain officers to give security.

SEC. 11. The recorder, treasurer and marshal, shall, respectively, before they enter upon the discharge of the duties of their respective offices, give such security for the faithful performance thereof, and trusts reposed in them, as shall be prescribed by the ordinances of said city.

General powers of common council.

SEC. 12. The common council shall have power to organize, maintain and regulate a police of the city, and to make all such by-laws and ordinances as they shall deem necessary for the preservation of the public peace; for the prevention and dispersion of disorderly assemblies; for the suppression of riots; for the apprehension and punishment of vagrants, drunkards and disorderly persons; to suppress all disorderly houses, [houses] of ill-fame, and houses of assignation, and to punish the inmates and keepers thereof; to prohibit every species of gaming; to prevent the selling or giving away of any spirituous or fermented liquors to any drunkard, minor or apprentice; to regulate the keeping of gunpowder, and to prevent the discharge of every species of firearms; to prevent the violation of the Sabbath, and the disturbance of any religious congregation, or any other public meeting assembled for any lawful purpose; to provide against and punish immoderate riding or driving in any of the streets of the city; relative to a city watch; relative to the public lighting of said city with gas or otherwise; relative to the restraining of swine, cattle, horses, and other descriptions of animals, from running at large in the streets, lanes or alleys, and other public places in said city; relative to billiard and other tables, and pin or ball-alleys, kept for hire, gain or reward in said city; to establish and regulate one or more pounds for said city; for the punishment of all lewd and lascivious behavior in the streets and other public places in said city; to prevent and prohibit the encumbering the streets, side-walks, alleys, or public grounds, or squares; to provide for clearing the Kalamazoo and Battle Creek, and any other natural or artificial water-course in said city, of all wood, filth or other nuisances, and to probibit and prevent the depositing therein of all filthy and other matter, tending to render the water thereof impure, unwholesome or offensive; to regulate all graveyards belonging to the city, and the burial of the dead therein; to compel the occupants of lots to clear the sidewalks in front and adjacent thereto, of snow, ice, dirt, mud, boxes, and every incumbrance or obstruction thereon; to prohibit and prevent the running at large of dogs, to require them to be muzzled, and to authorize their destruction when running at large in violation of any ordinance of the common council; to prohibit, prevent, abate and remove all nuisances in said city, and punish the persons occasioning the same, and declare what shall be considered nuisances, and direct and authorize their speedy or immediate abatement or removal by the marshal of said city; and, if in order to abate or remove any nuisance, the common council shall deem it necessary to fill up, level or drain any lot or premises, they shall have power so to do, to assess the costs and expenses of such filling up, leveling or draining, and impose the same as an assessment or tax on said lot or premises, which shall be a lien thereon until paid, and shall be collected in the same manner as other taxes and assessments levied and imposed by the authority of the common council; to compel the owner or occupant of any grocery, soap or candle factory, butcher's shop, stall, stable, barn, privy, sewer, or other unwholesome or nauseous house or place, to cleanse or remove the same, whenever necessary for the comfort, health or convenience of the inhabitants of said city.

Ib.

Powers of common council relative to fires, &c.

SEC. 13. The common council shall have power and authority to make all such by-laws and ordinances as shall be necessary to secure said city and the inhabitants thereof against [injuries] by fire, thieves, robbers, burglars, and other persons violating the public peace; to compel the owners or occupants of buildings to procure and keep in readiness such number of fire-buckets as they may direct. They shall also have power to prohibit, forbid and prevent the construction or erection, within such parts, streets or districts of said city, as in their opinion the public safety may require, any wooden or frame house, store, shop, or other building, and prohibit and prevent the removing of wooden or frame buildings from any part of said city to any lot or place within said limits, and the re-building and repairing the same; and also to regulate the construction of party walls, chimneys, fire-places, and the putting up of stoves, stove-pipes, and other things that

Erection of buildings.

Party walls, chimneys, stoves, &c.

may be dangerous in causing or promoting fires; to prohibit and prevent the burning out of chimneys, and compel and regulate the cleaning the same, and to appoint one or more officers to enter into all buildings to discover whether the same are in a dangerous state, and to cause such as are in a dangerous state to be put in a safe condition; and also to regulate the construction of all blacksmith shops, cooper shops, carpenter shops, planing establishments, bakeries, and all buildings and establishments usually regarded as extra hazardous in respect to fire; to establish, maintain and regulate all such fire-engine, hook and ladder, and hose and bucket companies as they may deem expedient; to construct reservoirs, and provide such companies with necessary and proper buildings, engines and other implements to prevent and extinguish fires, and to appoint from among the inhabitants of said city such number of men willing to accept as may be deemed necessary and proper to be employed as firemen: *Provided*, Such number does not exceed one hundred for each company; and each fire, and hose, and hook and ladder company shall have the power to elect their own officers, and to pass by-laws for the organization and government of said company, and the members of the several companies shall have power to elect their chief and assistant chief engineers, subject to the approval of the common council, and may impose and collect such fines for the non-attendance or neglect of duty of any of its members as may be established by the by-laws and regulations of every such company; and every person belonging to such company may obtain from the recorder of said city a certificate to that effect, which shall be evidence thereof; and the members of any such company, during their continuance as such, shall be exempt from all duty in the militia in time of peace, and also from serving on any jury in any of the courts in this State, or payment of poll tax; and it shall be the duty of every fire company to take reasonable care of the fire-engines, hose-carts, hose, ladders, and other instruments used by said company, and in no case, by wrongful act or neglect, doing or permitting injury thereto, and

Power to enter and examine buildings.

Blacksmith shops, &c.

Fire companies.

Proviso.

Number limited.

By-laws of Fire companies.

Certificates of membership.

Exemption.

Duties of fire companies.

upon any alarm or breaking out of any fire within said city, each fire company shall forthwith assemble at the place of said fire, with the engine and other implements of each of said fire companies, and to be subject to the orders of the chief engineer of the fire department. And it shall be the duty of each fire company to assemble once in each month, or as often as may be directed by the common council, for the purpose of working or examining said engines and other implements, with a view to their perfect order and repair. Ib.

SEC. 14. Upon the breaking out of any fire in said city, the marshal shall immediately repair to the place of such fire, and aid and assist as well in extinguishing the fire as preventing any goods or property from being stolen or injured, and in protecting, removing and securing the same; and for which purpose, and as chief of the police, and the mayor, recorder, or any alderman may require the assistance of all bystanders, and in the pursuance of his duties, the marshal shall, in all respects, be obedient to the mayor, recorder and aldermen, or either of them, or such of them as may be present at such fire; and in case any bystander shall willfully refuse or neglect to comply with such requirements, he shall be punished in the manner provided by the by-laws or ordinances of the common council, who are hereby authorized to pass such by-laws in relation thereto as they may deem necessary. Duties of marshal in case of fire. Bystanders required to assist. Refusal, how punished.

SEC. 15. The common council shall have power, and it shall be their duty to adopt measures for the preservation of the public health of said city; to restrain or prohibit the slaughtering of animals within the limits of said city, and also the exercise of any unwholesome or dangerous avocation within said limits; to establish a board of health, and invest it with such powers, and impose upon it such duties as shall be necessary to secure said city and the inhabitants thereof from contagious, malignant and infectious diseases; to provide for its proper organization, and the election or the appointment of the necessary officers therefor, and make such by-laws, rules and regulations for its government and support as shall be required for en- Public health of city. Board of health established.

forcing the most prompt and efficient performance of its duties, and the lawful exercise of its powers.

Provisions relative to sewers, drains, bridges, &c. SEC. 16. The common council shall have full power and authority to construct, repair and preserve sewers, drains and reservoirs, and to provide for supplying such reservoirs with water; and to cause bridges to be built or repaired; to make by-laws and ordinances to regulate the Hay. weighing of hay, and the measuring of fire-wood, and for Fire wood. that purpose may appoint some proper person to measure all fire-wood brought into the city for the purpose of sale Drays, hacks &c. in the streets or public grounds; and also relative to drays, carts, hacks and other vehicles kept for the transportation of persons and property in said city, and prescribe the amount of charges for their services, and to designate the stands for the sale of hay, wood, produce and other things exposed for sale in the streets or public grounds, and also City market. for the location and regulation of a city market, and to impose a tariff or tax on all or any property brought into Powers, duties, compensation, &c., of officers. said city for sale; also relative to the powers, duties and compensation of the officers of said corporation, subject to the restrictions contained in this act; relative to the calling Meeting of electors. of meetings of the electors of the city; and also to provide for taking a census of the inhabitants of said city whenever the common council shall see fit, and to direct Licenses. and regulate the same; relative to the licensing of show-Showmen. men and other exhibitions where money or other consideration is demanded or received for admission, and to fix the Amount of license. amount of said license; also relative to the licensing of auctioneers, and to determine the amount of such license; to License of auctioneers. direct the number of and license inn-keepers and common Fines and penalties. victualers; to provide for the collection and disposition of all fines and penalties which may be incurred under the by-laws and ordinances of said city; to regulate the setting of Posts, shade trees, &c. awning and other posts, and shade trees, in the streets and other public places in said city; to designate in which of the streets of said city teams and vehicles shall not stand or remain; to cause the streets to be paved, and also to Sidewalks. cause side-walks and cross-walks to be constructed and repaired when and where they shall deem necessary and proper, and cause the expenses of paving said streets, or constructing or repairing such side-walks to be assessed on the lots or premises adjoining such streets or side-walks, and may pass all needful by-laws and ordinances in relation to the assessment and collection of the expenses therefor. They may also fix and establish the grades of all such streets and side-walks, and also establish lines upon which buildings may be erected, and beyond which such buildings shall not extend, and to make all such other by-laws and ordinances as they may deem proper and necessary for the safety, order and good government of said city, and to promote the prosperity and improve the condition of the inhabitants thereof, not inconsistent with the laws and constitution of this State, and the constitution of the United States; and to impose fines, forfeitures and penalties on all persons offending against the by-laws and ordinances made as aforesaid: *Provided*, That no by-law or ordinance shall impose a fine exceeding one hundred dollars, nor subject the offender to imprisonment in the county jail or city prison, as the case may be, exceeding ninety days: AND PROVIDED FURTHER, *That no by-law or ordinance shall be of any effect until the same shall have been published for two weeks successively in all the newspapers printed in said city, unless otherwise directed by a vote of two-thirds of all the members of the common council present.*

Grades of streets.

General regulations.

Proviso.

Amount of fine limited.

Proviso.

SEC. 17. The common council shall have full power to lay out, establish, open, extend, widen, straighten, alter, close, vacate or abolish any highways, streets, avenues, lanes, alleys, public grounds, or spaces in said city, whenever they shall deem it a necessary public improvement. And private property may be taken therefor, but the necessity for using such property, the just compensation to be made for the same, and the damage arising to any person from the making of said improvement, shall be ascertained by a jury of twelve free holders residing in said city.

Powers of common council relative to streets, &c.

Compensation for private property.

SEC. 18. Whenever the common council shall deem any such improvement necessary, they shall so declare,

Proceedings when private property is taken.

by resolution, which shall be drawn by the city attorney, and in said resolution, shall describe the contemplated improvement, and if they intend to take private property therefor, they shall declare such intention and describe such property in said resolution, with particularity sufficient for an ordinary conveyance thereof; and further declare that they will, on some day to be named in said resolution, apply to a justice of the peace of said city, for the drawing of a jury to ascertain the necessity for using the property intended to be taken, if it be intended to take any for such improvement, to ascertain the just damages and compensation which any person may be entitled to, if such intended improvement be made, and to apportion and assess such damages and compensation to and upon all the taxable property of said city; and the time to be named for applying to such justice shall be on a day subsequent to the required publication of said resolution.

Jury.

Common council to give notice.

SEC. 19. The common council shall give notice of the intended improvements, and of their intended application to such justice, by causing a copy of said resolution, certified by the recorder of the city, to be published once in each week for four successive weeks in all the newspapers of the city, and the marshal shall also give notice of said resolution by delivering a notice thereof, with a copy of the same annexed, to the owner or owners, or agent of any private property intended to be taken, if they can be found in said city, which notice shall be directed to them, or if they cannot be found, by leaving the same at their place of residence in said city, with some person of proper age. If they, or their place of residence in said city cannot be found, and such property be occupied, said notice and copy of said resolution shall be served by delivering the same to the occupant or occupants, or by leaving the same at their place of residence in said city, with some person of proper age; but if the owner or owners, or agents of such property, or their place of residence cannot be found, and it be not occupied, but they, their place of residence and that of the occupant or occupants cannot be found, or if the owner or owners, occupant or oc-

Notice to be served on owners.

cupants be unknown or non-residents of said city, then, in either such cases, notice of such resolution may be given by posting the same with a copy of said resolution in some conspicuous place upon the property intended to be taken. The marshal shall give notice of said resolution as above directed, and make return of his doings, and of the manner of giving said notice, as soon as practicable after the passage thereof, which return shall be made by [to] said justice of the peace at least six days before the day appointed in said resolution for the hearing of said application; and all persons interested therein, after notice given in the manner aforesaid, shall take notice of, and be bound by all subsequent proceedings without any further notice except as herein otherwise provided.

Marshal to make return

Persons interested bound by the proceedings.

SEC. 20. The recorder of the city shall deliver to the city attorney a certified copy of said resolution of the common council, whose duty it shall be to appear before said justice and make the application therein referred to, and conduct all further proceedings thereon in behalf of the common council.

Recorder to furnish copy to common council.

SEC. 21. Upon the day designated in said resolution, or some other day to be appointed by the said justice, and on filing a copy of said resolution and an affidavit showing the required publication thereof, the marshal shall attend before said justice and write down the names of twenty-four disinterested free holders residing in said city, and who shall be approved by said justice as such disinterested free holders and residents, and as qualified to serve as jurors.

Drawing jury.

SEC. 22. Said justice of the peace shall then issue a writ of summons directed to said marshal, commanding him to summons said twenty-four persons to be and appear before said justice to serve as jurors on some day to be named therein, which shall not be less than seven days after the issuing thereof. The marshal shall serve said summons at least three days before the return day thereof, and make return in the same manner as in the case of a summons for jurors in civil cases before justices of the peace, and the persons thus summoned shall be bound to

Ib.

attend before said justice and serve until discharged; and said justice shall impose upon them a fine not exceeding five dollars for each day's non-attendance before him, or neglect to serve, but they may be exempted and excused by the justice from serving for the same reasons for which jurors in civil cases may be exempted or excused.

Fines for non-attendance.

Selection of jurors.

SEC. 23. The names of the jurors in attendance, and who do not claim to be exempted, or are not excused from serving, shall then be written by the said justice, on separate slips of paper of equal size and appearance as near as practicable, and be deposited by him in a box having a lid or cover. He shall then shake said box so as thoroughly to mix said slips of paper, and shall draw out impartially and openly, so many of said slips of paper or ballots containing names written thereon, one after another, as shall be sufficient to form a jury of twelve persons. The right of challenge shall be allowed as in civil cases under the laws of this State.

Challenge allowed.

Proceedings in case of deficiency.

SEC. 24. If, in consequence of jurors being exempted, excused or set aside, there shall not be in the box any ballots, or sufficient number of ballots from which to draw the jury, the marshal shall forthwith, under the order of the justice, summons such further number of free holders of said city as the said justice shall deem necessary, and may order them to be and appear before said justice to serve as jurors, and the persons thus summoned shall be returned, be bound to attend before said justice and serve, and be competent to form the jury in the same manner and to the same effect as those first summoned.

Oath of jurors.

SEC. 25. The first twelve persons who shall appear as their names are drawn and called by said justice, or who are called by him when all the ballots have been drawn from the box, and shall be approved by said justice as qualified, shall be the jury, and be sworn to discharge their duties faithfully and according to the best of their abilities. Said justice shall then instruct said jury as to their duties and the law applicable to the case, and deliver to them a copy of the resolution of the common council as filed with him, and the city attorney shall give said

Instruction to jury.

jury legal advice and counsel concerning their duties whenever requested. Legal advice.

SEC. 26. The jury shall go to the place of the intended improvement, and upon, or as near as practicable to any property intended to be taken and described in said resolution, or as the case may be, which will be damaged if the intended improvement be made. Jury to view the premises.

SEC. 27. Said jury shall then ascertain the necessity for using the property intended to be taken, if it be intended to take any for such improvement, and if they shall find in the affirmative, they shall next determine the just damages and compensation to be paid to the owner or owners of any property intended to be taken for, or that may be damaged by the intended improvement, and award to the owner or owners thereof such damages and compensation as they shall deem just. Jury to ascertain and determine and award damages. If such property shall be subject to a valid mortgage, lease and agreement, or to either, and such facts shall be made to appear to the jury, then said jury shall apportion and award to the owners of such property, the parties in interest to such mortgage, lease and agreement, or to either of them, such portions of the damages and compensation as they shall deem just; Proceedings when property is encumbered. and in all cases when any such damages and compensation shall be awarded, the same shall be payable out of the city treasury, and the means therefor shall be raised from time to time as may be necessary with the general city taxes. Damages, how paid.

SEC. 28. The word "alley," as used in this act, shall be construed to mean only those ways or passages which bisect or divide the interior of a block. Meaning of alley. No alley shall be opened except upon petition of the owners of a majority of the lots on the block or blocks to be intersected thereby, and upon security being given to indemnify the city against the expenses of opening said alleys. How opeued.

SEC. 29. Said jury after completing the aforesaid duties shall then make in writing, and each shall sign the same, a report to said justice of their doings, enclose the same in a sealed envelope and file it with said justice within thirty days after they were sworn. Report of jury, when made.

What report shall contain.

SEC. 30. In cases where said jury shall find such improvement to be necessary, they shall state in their report the just damages and compensation ascertained and awarded by them to the owner of any private property, or to any person claiming an interest therein by virtue of any valid mortgage, lease or agreement, to which such property may be subject, together with the names of such owner or claimant, if known, and a description of the property intended to be taken. In case any damages and compensation be awarded to any person claiming an interest in such property by virtue of a valid mortgage, lease or agreement, to which such property may be subject, it shall be sufficient to state further in such case the name of said claimant, the date of such mortgage, lease or agreement, or assignment thereof, if there be any, by virtue of which such claimant has an interest in the property intended to be taken.

Further proceedings.

SEC. 31. Said report may be confirmed by said justice, and he shall appoint some day when he will consider said report, and objections against the confirmation thereof, on the part of all persons interested therein, whereof the city attorney shall give notice by publishing the same in all the newspapers of said city once in each week, for two successive weeks, and he shall file with such justice an affidavit of such publication before the time appointed for considering said report.

Objections.

Said objections shall be filed with said justice in writing, but may be argued, and the consideration of said report and objections may be adjourned from time to time, until said report be confirmed, or otherwise disposed of, as herein provided.

Objections to be of law and real.

SEC. 32. Said report shall not be annulled for objections as to matters of form; all objections shall be objections of law, and to matters of substance, but the damages and compensation to be paid to any person may be inquired into, if objected to as being excessively large or inadequately small.

Jury to review if report be not confirmed.

SEC. 33. If no objections be filed on or before the day appointed by said justice for the consideration of said report, the said report shall be confirmed; but if objections be filed, said justice, after considering the same, shall confirm or annul said report on all questions of law, and shall refer it back to the same jury, for the purpose of reviewing and correcting all errors in matter of fact therein contained, whenever necessary, and making any alteration thereof which said jury may deem just or necessary; and thereon said jury shall review, correct or alter said report in manner aforesaid, and shall return and file the same with said justice within five days after said report was referred back to them as aforesaid, and thereupon said justice shall confirm or annul said report.

Provision for another jury in certain cases.

SEC. 34. If said report be annulled, or the jury cannot agree, or from death, sickness or any other cause, shall fail to make a report within the thirty days required above, the justice may, on the application of the city attorney, designate some day when another jury may be had; and such other jury shall be obtained, drawn, summoned, returned, bound to attend and serve, have the same qualifications, be sworn, and, when sworn, have the same powers and duties as the first jury. The same proceedings, after they are sworn, shall be had by them, and by and before said justice, as provided for above, after the first jury is sworn.

Vacancy, how filled.

SEC. 35. If any juror, after being sworn shall die, or from sickness or any other cause, be unable to discharge his duties as such juror, said justice may appoint another person to serve in his place, who shall be sworn, and shall have the like qualifications, powers and duties, as those already sworn.

Original party may appeal.

SEC. 36. Any person to whom damages and compensation may be awarded for any of his property intended to be taken, or on account of the intended improvement, considering himself aggrieved, may appeal from the judgment of the said justice confirming the report of the jury, to the circuit court for the county of Calhoun, by filing in writing with said justice a notice of such appeal and specification of the errors complained of within five days after the confirmation of said report by said justice, and serving within the same time a copy of said notice and specifi-

Appeal, how made.

Bond.

cation of errors on the city attorney, and filing a bond with said justice, to be approved by him, conditioned for the prosecution of said appeal, and the payment of all costs that may be awarded against the appellant, in case the judgment of confirmation of said justice be affirmed.

Duty of justice in relation to appeal.

SEC. 37. In case of appeal as above, it shall be the duty of said justice, within ten days thereafter, to make and transmit to the clerk of said circuit court a certified copy of all the proceedings in the case, which shall be filed by said clerk in his office.

Proceedings on appeal.

SEC. 38. The said circuit court, at any term thereof, shall, with the least practicable delay, hear and try the matter of said appeal, and may affirm or reverse the judgment of the said justice confirming the report of the jury; but the same shall not be reversed for matter of form, nor for any errors, except errors of law, and only in regard to the appellant or appellants. The court shall give judgment for reasonable costs and expenses in the matter of said appeal and the proceedings thereon to be taxed, and all costs and expenses awarded to the city of Battle Creek, in case of affirmation, shall be applied on and deducted from the damages and compensation, if any, to be paid to the appellant or appellants.

Expenses, by whom paid.

Proceedings may be remanded to justice in certain cases.

SEC. 39. If there be a reversal for any errors which it is practicable for said justice or said jury to correct, with due regard to the public interest and the rights of individuals, the proceedings shall be remanded to said justice, with directions that such error be corrected, said justice (or as the case may be), said jury under the direction of said justice, shall correct such error, and thereupon the report of the jury shall be confirmed by said justice, without any further right of appeal.

Common council may elect to pay damages in certain cases.

SEC. 40. In every case of annulment of the report of the jury by said justice, or reversal by the circuit court, the common council, in behalf of said city, may, by resolution, elect to pay the damages and compensation claimed by said appellant or appellants. On filing a certified copy of said resolution with said justice within twenty days after the annulment or reversal, the report of said jury shall be reviewed and confirmed by said justice, as to all persons interested therein, except the objector, appellant or appellants, and without any further right of appeal. If the common council do not elect, as above provided, all the proceedings shall be null and void, and no further proceedings shall be had, except in a case of reversal, when the proceedings may have been remanded to said justice for the correction of certain errors, in which case such errors shall be corrected, and the report of the jury confirmed as above provided. When proceedings to be void.

SEC. 41. If the report of the jury be confirmed by said justice in any case above provided for, or if the judgment of confirmation be affirmed on appeal to the circuit court, such confirmation shall be final and conclusive as to all persons interested therein. When confirmation to be final.

SEC. 42. When the report of the jury shall have been thus finally confirmed, or the judgment of confirmation affirmed by the circuit court, said justice shall prepare a certified copy of the report of the jury as confirmed by said justice, and of the order of the justice confirming the same, and deliver the same to the recorder of said city, who shall file the same in his office, and shall record the same at length in a book to be provided, used and known as a book of street records; such certified copy, such record, or a like copy made and certified by the recorder, shall, in all courts and places, be presumptive evidence of the matters therein contained, and of the regularity of all proceedings from the commencement thereof to the order of the justice or of the circuit court, as the case may be, confirming the report of the jury. Copy of report filed in recorder's office. Certified copy to be evidence.

SEC. 43. Within sixty days after the confirmation of the report of the jury, or after the judgment of confirmation on appeal, be affirmed, the common council shall pay or tender to the respective persons the several amounts of damages and compensation awarded to them according to the report of the jury as confirmed or elected, as above provided for, to be paid by the common council, and in case any such person shall refuse the same, be unknown, or a non-resident of said city, or for any reason incapacita- Damages to be tendered.

ted from receiving his or her amount, or the right thereto be disputed or doubtful, the common council may deposit the amount awarded in such case or elected to be paid by the common council, in the treasury of the city, to the credit of any person entitled thereto, and shall, on demand, pay the same over to any person competent and entitled to receive it.

May be deposited in city treasury in certain cases.

The property taken becomes city property.

SEC. 44. Upon such payment, tender or deposit in the city treasury, the premises or property so intended to be taken and described in said resolution, shall become a public highway, or as the case may be, the property of said city for the uses and purposes for which it was taken, and the common council may enter upon, take possession of and convert the same to the uses and purposes for which it was taken; a certificate of the city treasurer of such tender, payment or deposit, or record thereof in the book of street records, or certified copy of such record, shall, in all courts and places, be presumptive evidence of the facts therein stated, of the vesting of the fee of the property taken in the city of Battle Creek, and of the right of the common council to take possession of and convert the same to the uses for which it was taken.

What shall be evidence.

When certain covenants shall be discharged.

SEC. 45. In all cases when any real estate subject to any lease or agreement shall be taken as aforesaid, all the covenants and stipulations contained therein shall cease, determine and be discharged upon the final confirmation of the report of the jury, or upon the affirmation by the circuit court of the judgment of confirmation. If a part only of such real estate be taken, said covenants and stipulations shall cease, determine and be discharged only as to such part; and said justice, on application of any party in interest to such lease or agreement, and after a notice thereof of eight days in writing to the other parties in interest, may appoint three disinterested residents and freeholders of said city, commissioners to determine the rents and payments to be thereafter paid, and the covenants, stipulations or conditions thereafter to be performed under such lease or agreement in respect to the residue or part of such real estate not taken; said commissioners shall

Commissioners appointed.

before entering upon their duties, take and subscribe an oath to be administered by said justice, faithfully to discharge their duties, which oath shall be filed with said justice. Said three commissioners shall make and sign a report in writing of their doings to said justice, which shall be filed by and with him, within thirty days after their appointment; and said report, on being confirmed by said justice, shall be binding and conclusive on the parties in interest to such lease or agreement.

Oath.

Commissioners to report within thirty days.

SEC. 46. The common council shall pay said jury such compensation for their services as they may deem just, and they shall have power to abandon or discontinue such proceedings before said justice at any time before the final confirmation of the report of the jury.

Compensation of jury

SEC. 47. The mayor of said city shall be the chief executive officer thereof. It shall be his duty, in addition to the other requirements of this act, to see that all the officers of said city faithfully comply with and discharge their official duties, to see that all laws pertaining to the municipal government of said city, and all ordinances and resolutions of the common council be faithfully observed and executed. He is also hereby authorized and empowered generally to administer oaths and take affidavits, and shall from time to time recommend such measures to the common council as to him shall seem proper.

Mayor of city, his powers and duties.

SEC. 48. The recorder of said city shall, in addition to the other duties hereby imposed upon him, keep the corporation seal, and all papers filed in or pertaining to his office; shall make and preserve a record of all ordinances and by-laws passed by said common council, in proper books to be provided therefor; and when requested, shall duly certify, under the corporate seal, copies of all the records of said common council, and all papers duly filed in his office, which shall be evidence in all places of the matters therein contained; also perform such duties as are or may be required of township clerks, in all cases which he is authorized or required by this act, or the laws of this State, to perform the duties of township clerk; and for such services he shall receive the same fees as they

Recorder, his powers and duties.

Recorder's certificate to be evidence.

Fees.

are entitled to receive under the laws of this State; he is also hereby authorized and empowered generally to administer oaths and to take affidavits.

Marshal, his powers and duties.

SEC. 49. The marshal of said city shall be chief of the police of said city, and it shall be his duty to serve all processes that may be lawfully delivered to him for service; to see that all the by-laws and ordinances of the common council are promptly and efficiently enforced; he shall obey all the lawful orders of the mayor or the common council, and shall also attend the meetings of the common council, and may command the aid and assistance of all constables and all other persons in the discharge of the duties imposed upon him by law, and shall be a peace officer; he shall also under the direction of the common council, see to the making, grading, paving, repairing and opening of all streets, lanes, alleys, bridges, side-walks and cross-walks within said city, unless the common council shall devolve the same upon one or more of the deputy street commissioners that they are hereby authorized to appoint; he shall have power and authority, and it shall be his duty, with or without process, to apprehend any person found disturbing the peace or offending against any of the by-laws and ordinances of the city, and forthwith take such person before any justice of the peace of said city, to be dealt with as the by-laws and ordinances or this act shall provide, and may apprehend and imprison any person found drunk in the street until such person shall become sober, and shall be authorized to command the assistance, in the discharge of such duties, of any of the citizens, if deemed by him necessary; and he shall perform all the duties that may be required of him by the by-laws or ordinances passed by the said common council.

City treasurer to have custody of money, &c., belonging to city.

SEC. 50. The treasurer of said city shall have the custody of all the money and evidences of value belonging to the city; he shall receive all moneys belonging to and receivable by the corporation, and keep an accurate account of all receipts and expenditures thereof; he shall pay no money out of the treasury, except in pursuance of and by authority of law, and upon a warrant signed by

Warrants for money, by whom signed. — To make exhibits to common council on demand. — To make financial statement. — To collect city taxes, &c., in like manner as township treasurers.

the recorder and countersigned by the mayor, which shall specify the purpose for which the amount is to be paid; he shall keep an accurate account of, and be charged with moneys received for each fund of the corporation, and shall pay every warrant out of the particular fund constituted or raised for the purpose for which said warrant was issued, and having the name of such fund endorsed thereon by the recorder. He shall exhibit to the common council annually, and as often and for such periods as may be required by them, a full and detailed account of all receipts and expenditures since the date of his last annual report, classifying them by the fund to which such receipts are credited, and out of which such expenditures are made, and shall also, when required, exhibit a general statement showing the financial condition of the treasury, which account, report and statement shall be filed in the office of the recorder; he shall also collect all city taxes imposed by the common council in the manner provided by this act and the by-laws and ordinances in relation thereto; it shall also be his duty, and he is hereby authorized to perform the same duties in relation to the collection and return of taxes for State, county and school purposes, assessed and levied within said city, as is or shall be required of township treasurers, and shall perform the same in the same manner, under like instructions, and under the same liabilities that are imposed by law upon such township treasurers.

Supervisor, his powers and duties. — Fees.

SEC. 51. The supervisor is hereby authorized and required to perform the same duties that the supervisors of townships, under the general laws of this State, are required to perform in relation to the assessing of property and levying of taxes for State, county and school purposes, and he shall also issue his warrant to the treasurer of said city for the collection of such taxes in the same manner as the supervisors of townships issue warrants to the treasurers of townships for the collection thereof, and for such services he shall receive the same fees as supervisors are entitled to; he shall also represent said city in the board of supervisors of the said county of Calhoun, and shall be entitled to all the rights, privileges and powers of the members of said board of supervisors.

Justices of the peace.

SEC. 52. The justices of the peace elected under the provisions of this act shall have the like powers and jurisdiction, and be subject to the same duties and liabilities, as are or shall be provided by law in relation to the powers, and duties, and liabilities of justices of the peace of the several townships of this State.

Certain other officers.

SEC. 53. The school inspectors, directors of the poor, and constables, elected under the provisions of this act, shall perform the duties, receive the compensation, and be subject to the liabilities which are or shall be by law provided for the corresponding offices respectively of the townships of this State, and said constables shall also be peace officers.

Powers of justices of the peace.

SEC. 54. Any justice of the peace of said city is hereby authorized and empowered to inquire of, hear, try and determine, in a summary manner, all the offences which shall be committed within the limits of said city, against any of the by-laws or ordinances which shall be made by the common council in pursuance of the powers granted by this act; to punish the offenders as by the said by-laws or ordinances shall be prescribed or directed; to award all processes, and to take recognizances for the keeping of the peace, for the appearance of the person charged, and upon appeal and to commit to prison as occasion shall lawfully require.

Prosecutions, how commenced and conducted.

SEC. 55. In all prosecutions for a violation of any of the by-laws or ordinances passed by the said common council, upon complaint being made upon oath before said justice, setting forth therein the substance of the offence complained of, such justice of the peace shall issue a warrant in the name of the people of the State of Michigan for the apprehension of the offender, directed to the marshal of the city of Battle Creek, or any constable of the county of Calhoun (except in the cases mentioned in the next succeeding section), and such process may be executed by any of said officers anywhere within the county of Calhoun, and shall be returnable the same as other similar process issued by justices of the peace, that upon bringing the person so charged before said justice of the peace, he shall plead to said complaint, and in case of his refusing to plead thereto, or standing mute, the said justice of the peace shall enter the plea of not guilty for the person so charged; that upon said complaint and plea a trial shall be had; and upon conviction of said offender, and the imposition of a fine, it shall be the duty of the justice to issue an execution, directed to the marshal of said city, or any constable of said county of Calhoun, commanding him to collect of the goods and chattels of the person so offending the amount of such fine with interest and cost; and for the want of goods and chattels wherewith to satisfy the same, that [he take] the body of the defendant and commit him to the common jail of said county, or to the city prison of said city, in the discretion of said court, and the sheriff or the keeper of said city prison shall safely keep the body of the person so committed, until he be discharged by due course of law; and in case where imprisonment alone shall be imposed upon the person so convicted, the said justice shall issue a commitment, directed as aforesaid, commanding his commitment until the expiration of the time for which he shall be sentenced to imprisonment, or until he be discharged by due course of law; and in case where both fine and imprisonment are imposed upon the person so convicted by the judgment of such justice of the peace, he shall issue the necessary process to carry such judgment into effect; and it shall be lawful to use the common jail of said county for the imprisonment of all persons liable to imprisonment under the by-laws and ordinances of the common council; and all persons committed by any justice for the violation thereof, shall be in the custody of the sheriff of said county or the keeper of said city prison, who shall safely keep the person so committed until lawfully discharged as in other cases: *Provided*, That the common council may remit any such fine, in whole or in part, if it shall be made to appear that the person so imprisoned is unable to pay the same: *Provided further*, That all costs and expenses incurred

Execution to issue on conviction.

The body taken for want of goods.

Commitment to issue.

Sheriff to have custody of prisoners.

Common council may remit fine.

Expenses, how paid. under the provisions of this section shall be provided for and paid out of the city treasury.

Proceedings as to offenders who have escaped from the country. SEC. 56. Whenever any person or persons charged with having violated any of the ordinances of the common council, by which the offender is liable to imprisonment, shall have escaped from the county, or shall reside or be without the limits thereof, any justice of the peace residing in said city to whom complaint shall be made, shall issue a warrant in the name of the people of the State of Michigan, directed to the Sheriff of any county in this State, commanding him forthwith to bring the body of such person or persons before him to be dealt with according to law; and every sheriff to whom said warrant shall be delivered for service, is hereby required to execute the same under the penalties which are incurred by law by sheriffs and other officers for neglecting or refusing to execute criminal process.

Jury may be demanded. SEC. 57. In all trials before any justice of the peace, under the provisions of this act, of any person or persons charged with any violation of any by-law or ordinance of the common council, he or they shall be entitled to a trial by a jury of six persons, and all the proceedings for selecting and summoning such jury, and in the trial of the cause, shall be in conformity, as near as may be, with the mode of proceedings in similar cases before justices of the peace, and within the same time, and in all cases the right of appeal from the justice's court to the circuit court for said county of Calhoun, shall be allowed to the parties, and the same recognizance or bond shall be given as is or may be required by law in appeals from justice's courts in similar cases.

Right of appeal.

Bond.

Fines, how disposed of. SEC. 58. All fines recovered for a violation of any by-law or ordinance of said common council, shall be paid to the treasurer of said city by the officer receiving the same immediately after the receipt thereof; and any person who shall refuse or neglect to pay the same as aforesaid, shall be deemed guilty of misdemeanor, and upon conviction thereof, shall be punished by a fine of not less than one hundred dollars, nor more than five hundred dollars,

Penalty.

or by imprisonment in the county jail not less than three months, nor more than one year, or by both such fine and imprisonment, in the discretion of the court.

No inhabitant deemed incompetent as witness or juror.

SEC. 59. In all suits or proceedings in which the corporation of the city of Battle Creek shall be a party or shall be interested, no inhabitant of said city shall be deemed incompetent as a witness or juror, on account of his interest in the event of such suit or action: *Provided*, Such interest be such only as he has in common with the inhabitants of said city.

Proviso.

Supervisor to make separate statement of taxable property.

SEC. 60. The supervisor of said city shall make out from the assessment roll, a separate list and statement of the valuation of all the taxable personal property and a description of all lots or parcels of land within said city, inserting in a separate part of such list, descriptions of lands owned by non-residents of said city, with the value of each lot or parcel set down opposite to such description as the same shall appear on the assessment roll; and if such lot or tract was not separately described in such roll, then in proportion to the valuation which shall have been affixed to the whole tract of which such a lot or parcel forms a part.

To make assessments of highway labor.

SEC. 61. It shall be the duty of said supervisor to make an estimate and assessment of highway labor to be laid out, performed, and expended in said city, and in making said estimate and assessment he shall proceed as follows:

Persons assessed one day.

1st. Every male inhabitant in said city being above the age of twenty-one and under the age of fifty years, except paupers, persons of color not possessing taxable property, idiots and lunatics, shall be assessed one day.

Residue of highway labor.

2d. The residue of the highway labor to be assessed, not exceeding one day's work upon one hundred dollars of the valuation, shall be apportioned upon the estate, real and personal, of every inhabitant in [said] city, and upon each tract or parcel of land therein of which the owners are non-residents, as the same shall appear by the assessment roll.

Names affixed.

3d. Said supervisor shall affix to the name of each person [against] whom highway labor is by him assessed as aforesaid, and not assessed upon said city assessment roll, and also to each valuation of property within said city, the number of days which such person or property shall be assessed for highway labor, adding one day to the assessment of each person liable to a poll tax, and assessed upon said city assessment roll.

Poll tax.

Recorder to act as clerk.

SEC. 62. The recorder of said city shall act as the clerk of said supervisor in making out said estimate and assessment of highway labor, and shall make duplicate lists thereof, which shall be subscribed by said supervisor, one of which lists shall be filed by such recorder in his office, and the other shall be forthwith delivered to the marshal of said city; and said highway labor shall be laid out, performed and expended by said marshal and the deputy street commissioners appointed by the common council, at such times, in such manner, and at such places as he or they shall, by resolution of the common council, be directed, and such marshal and street commissioner shall have the same power, and proceed in the same manner to enforce the performance of said highway labor, and to collect commutation money in case of the non-performance thereof, as is now or shall hereafter be provided by law in case of overseers of highways in townships, and all persons assessed for highway labor shall be entitled to commute therefor in the same manner and upon the same terms as is or shall be provided in townships.

To make and file duplicate lists.

Highway labor, how performed and expended.

Power of common council to levy and collect taxes limited.

SEC. 63. The common council shall also have power and authority to levy and collect taxes on all real and personal property within the limits of said city, by them deemed necessary, not exceeding the sum of five thousand dollars annually, for the period of five years from and after the time when this act shall take effect, and a sum not exceeding ten thousand dollars from and after the expiration of said five years; and shall [have] power and authority to make and establish all necessary by-laws and ordinances for the collection of the same, and every assessment of tax lawfully imposed by the said common council, on any lands, tenements, hereditaments or premises whatsoever in said city shall be and remain a lien on such lands, tene-

May establish by-laws for collection of taxes.

Taxes a lien until paid.

ments and hereditaments from the time of imposing such tax until paid, and the owner or occupant or parties interested respectively in said real estate, shall be liable, on demand, to pay every such tax to be levied as aforesaid.

Recorder to assess taxes.

SEC. 64. It shall be the duty of the recorder, [under] the direction of the common council, whenever the city assessment roll shall have been completed in each and every year, to assess the taxes that have been levied by the common council for the year, adding thereto, and to all other taxes required by law to be assessed by him, not more than four per cent for collecting expenses, upon the taxable property in the city, according and in proportion to the individual and particular estimate and valuation as specified in the assessment roll of the city for the year. He shall, thereupon, deliver to the city treasurer a copy of said assessment roll, with the taxes for the [year] annexed to each valuation and carried out in a column thereof; and if there be other taxes assessed than for the expenses of the city, they shall be carried out in separate columns, and carry out the total amount of taxes in the last column of said roll, and shall annex thereto a warrant, under the hands of the recorder and mayor, and the seal of said city, commanding the treasurer to collect from the several persons named in said roll the several sums mentioned in the last column thereof, opposite their respective names, on or before the day specified in such warrant; and it shall authorize the said treasurer, in case any person shall neglect or refuse to pay his tax, to levy the same by distress and sale of the goods and chattels of such person, in the same manner as is or shall be provided by law in case of township treasurers.

Expense for collecting limited.

A copy of roll to be delivered to city treasurer.

Warrant annexed.

Treasurer to collect taxes.

SEC. 65. The treasurer, upon receiving the tax-roll, shall proceed to collect the taxes therein mentioned, and shall for that purpose, call upon each person taxed, if a resident of the city, at least once, and demand payment of the taxes charged to him upon said roll; and in case of a refusal or neglect to pay such taxes, the treasurer shall levy the same by distress and sale of the goods and chattels of every such person, wherever found within the city, and

May sell property.

may take any property that can be taken by township treasurers, in the collection of taxes; he shall give the same notice, and shall sell in the same manner as township treasurers are required to do in the collection of taxes, and any surplus shall be returned to the person in whose possession said property was when the distress was made.

Tax roll; when returned.

The said treasurer shall, within ten days after the time mentioned in his warrant for the collection of said taxes, return said tax roll into the office of the recorder; and in case any of the taxes mentioned in said roll shall remain unpaid, and he shall be unable to collect the same, he shall make out a statement of the taxes remaining unpaid and due, with a full and perfect description of such premises from said roll, and shall attach thereto an affidavit that the sums mentioned in said statement remain unpaid, and that he has not, upon diligent inquiry, been able to discover any goods or chattels belonging to the person charged with or liable to pay such tax.

Unpaid taxes.

New warrant may issue for unpaid taxes.

SEC. 66. Whenever the treasurer shall not be able to collect any city tax on personal property, on account of the absence of the person so taxed, or for any other cause, the recorder may, if directed by the common council, issue a new warrant to the treasurer for such tax; and thereupon said warrant shall be and remain in full force for the purposes of such collection as long as shall be directed by the common council, and the treasurer shall charge interest on all such taxes at ten per cent per annum from the time of returning the tax roll until the day of collection; it shall be also lawful for the treasurer, in the name of the city, to sue the person or persons against whom any such personal property tax was assessed, after the return of the assessment roll before any court of competent jurisdiction, and to have, use and take all lawful ways and means provided by law for the collection of debts, to enforce the payment of any such tax. Executions issued upon judgments rendered for every such tax, may be levied upon any property liable to be seized and sold under warrants issued for the collection of any city taxes; and the proceedings of any officer with such execution shall be the

Interest charged.

Suits authorized.

Executions may issue.

same in all respects as is now or shall be hereafter directed by law. The production of any assessment roll on the trial of any action brought for the recovery of any tax therein assessed, may, upon proof that it is the original assessment roll, or the assessment roll with the warrant annexed, of the city, be read or used in evidence; and if it shall appear from said assessment roll that there is a tax therein assessed against the defendant in such suit, it shall be *prima facie* evidence of the legality and regularity of the assessment of the same; and the court before whom the case may be pending, shall proceed to render judgment against the defendant, unless he shall make it appear that he has paid such tax; and no stay of execution shall be allowed on any such judgment.

Assessment roll used as evidence.

Stay of execution not allowed.

SEC. 67. The recorder shall, immediately after receiving the said statement, transcribe the same into a book to be provided and kept for that purpose, and shall, under the direction of the common council, and in pursuance of the ordinances or resolutions of said council, proceed to sell at public sale so much of said lands so returned on account of the non-payment of the taxes thereon, as shall be necessary to satisfy the amount of taxes, together with such amount as shall be directed by the common council to cover the expenses of such sale, notice of which sale shall be given by publication in a newspaper published in said city, once in each week for four successive weeks preceding such sale; and the said recorder, on such sale, shall give to the purchaser or purchasers of any such lands, a certificate in writing, describing the lands purchased, and the time when the purchaser will be entitled to a deed for the same, and in case a less amount than the whole of any such description should be sold, the part so sold shall be taken from the north side or end thereof, and shall be bounded on the south by a line running due east and west: *Provided*, That if any parcel of land cannot be sold to any person for the taxes and charges, the recorder shall bid the same off to the common council of said city, and shall give a like certificate of such sale, which shall have the like effect in all respects as if the same had been given to any other

Recorder required to sell.

Notice of sale to be published.

Certificate to purchaser.

Proviso.

purchaser thereof. Upon the completion of said sale, the said recorder shall deliver to the treasurer a detailed statement of such sale, containing a description of the premises sold, the particular tax and amount for which the same were sold, and the names of the purchasers, which shall be transcribed in a book to be provided for and kept by said treasurer, and said recorder shall also pay to said treasurer, at the same time, all the moneys received upon such sales.

Statement delivered to treasurer.

Lands sold, when and how redeemable.

SEC. 68. Any person claiming any of the lands sold as aforesaid, or any interest therein, may, at any time within one year next succeeding the sale, redeem any parcel of said lands, or any part or interest in the same, by paying to the treasurer of said city the amount for which such parcel was sold, or such proportion thereof as the part or interest redeemed shall amount to, with interest thereon, at the rate of twenty-five per cent. per annum, fifteen per-cent. of which shall be paid to the purchaser; but in no case shall the interest be computed for a less time than three months, from the day of sale; whereupon the treasurer shall issue and deliver to the person making such payment a certificate of the redemption thereof; and he shall at the expiration of the year after the making of said sales deliver to the recorder of said city a statement of all the lands that have been redeemed as aforesaid, and the amounts paid for such redemption.

Statement of redemption delivered to recorder.

Deed to be executed.

SEC. 69. Upon the presentation of any such certificate of sale to the recorder after the expiration of the time for the redemption of the lands sold as aforesaid, he shall execute to the purchaser, his heirs or assigns, a conveyance of the lands [therein] described, which conveyance shall vest in the person or persons to whom it shall be given, an absolute estate, in fee simple, subject to all the claims the State may have thereon; and the same conveyance shall be *prima facie* evidence that the proceedings were regular, according to the provisions of this act, from the valuation of the same by the supervisor to the date of the deed, inclusive; and every such conveyance, duly made and acknowledged, may be given in evidence in all courts

Deed to be evidence that proceedings are regular.

of this State, in the same manner and with the like effect of any other conveyance of real estate, or any interest therein; and the common council may, upon satisfactory evidence, upon oath, of the payment of any tax upon real estate, and that the same has been returned for non-payment, by mistake or otherwise, improperly or for any other irregularity in the return of such real estate, cancel the certificate of sale, before the lands therein described has been conveyed as aforesaid; and thereupon the recorder shall draw an order upon the treasurer, countersigned by the mayor, for the amount of the purchase money, and no deed shall be given upon such certificate of sale. And every such deed, when witnessed and acknowledged in the manner prescribed by law for witnessing and acknowledging deeds in other cases, and after it shall have been on record two years in the office of the register of deeds, in and for said county of Calhoun, except: *First*, When the same shall be annulled according to law. *Second*, When the land sold was not subject to taxation at the date of the assessment of the taxes for which it was sold. *Third*, When the taxes have been paid to the proper officer within the time limited by law, for the payment or redemption thereof. Or, *Fourth*, When a certificate that no taxes were charged against the land, has been given by the proper officer, within the time limited by law for the payment or redemption thereof, shall be positive evidence that the lands therein described were, by such deed conveyed, in fee simple, to the grantee therein named, and his heirs and assigns. And no suit of ejectment shall be commenced to recover said lands, or title thereto sustained thereafter, by any person claiming or holding possession or title through any other source.

Provision to cancel certificate of sale.

Deed, properly executed and recorded.

With certain exceptions.

To be positive evidence.

Suit of ejectment precluded.

SEC. 70. The common council of said city is hereby authorized and required to perform the same duties in and for said city as are by law imposed upon the township boards of the several townships of this State in reference to schools, school taxes, county and State taxes, the support of the poor, the State, district and county elections, except as is otherwise provided by this act; the mayor and

Powers and duties of common council relative to schools, &c.

Taxes.

Support of poor.

Grand and petit jurors. recorder shall select and return lists of grand and petit jurors in the same manner and within the same time that the same duty is or shall be required of township officers in this State; and the supervisors, justices of the peace, recorder, school inspectors, directors of the poor, and all other officers of said city, who are required to perform the duties of township officers of this State, shall take the oath, give the bonds, perform like duties, and receive the same pay, and in the same manner, and be subject to the same liabilities, as is provided for the corresponding township officers, except as is otherwise provided in this act, or as may be provided by the ordinances of the common council.

Duties of certain officers.

Oath and bond.

Liabilities.

Compensation. SEC. 71. The recorder, marshal, deputy street commissioners, and all other officers of said city, shall receive such compensation for their services as the common council may deem right and proper, unless the same is fixed by the provisions of this act; but the mayor and aldermen shall receive no compensation for their services.

Common council to publish statement of money expended. SEC. 72. The common council shall, at least once in each and every year, cause to be published in at least one newspaper printed in said city, a just and true account of all the moneys received or expended by them in their corporate capacity during the year or other period next preceding such publication, and also the disposition thereof, previous to which they shall audit and settle the accounts of the city treasurer and the accounts of all other officers or persons having claims against the city, or accounts with it, and shall make out in detail a statement of all receipts and expenditures; and which statement shall fully specify all appropriations made by the common council, and the object and purpose for which the same were made, and the amount of money expended under such appropriations, the amount of taxes raised, the amount expended on highways and streets, and all such information as shall be necessary to a full and perfect understanding of the financial concerns of the city.

What statement shall specify.

Who to be temporary common council. SEC. 73. The president, clerk and justices [trustees] of the village of Battle Creek shall be the common council, and shall respectively discharge all the duties of mayor, recorder and aldermen of the city of Battle Creek, and all the other officers of said village shall be such officers of the city of Battle Creek, until others are elected and qualified in their stead, and all the by-laws, ordinances and other regulations of the common council of said village now in force, not inconsistent with this act or the provisions of the statutes of this State, shall be and remain in force until altered or repealed by the common council of said city of Battle Creek, and all the township officers of the townships of Battle Creek and Emmett, except justices of the peace residing in said city, may continue to discharge all the duties of such officers for said townships, until after the first Monday of March next.

Village ordinance to remain in force until repealed.

Term of township officers.

SEC. 74. No money shall be drawn from the treasury, unless in pursuance of previous appropriations specifying the purpose thereof; and any order or warrant directing or requiring the payment of the same, shall specify the object and purpose of such payment, and shall be signed by the recorder and countersigned by the mayor of said city.

Warrant for money; object to be specified.

SEC. 75. All the personal and real estates, rights, credits and effects whatsoever, and all and every right or interest therein belonging to the village of Battle Creek, and all demands due and to grow due to the same, shall hereafter fully and absolutely belong to the corporation created by this act, saving nevertheless, to all and every person his or their just rights therein, and to the end that all and singular the estates and rights aforesaid may be fully vested in the corporation hereby created, every person who is or shall be possessed thereof, shall deliver the same to the mayor, recorder and aldermen of the city of Battle Creek, with all moneys, deeds, evidences of debt, property, books and papers touching or concerning the same, when legally required so to do; and the said city may sue in its corporate name to recover any demand or debt due or to grow due to said village, and the corporation hereby created shall be liable for and pay all just debts due from or claims or demands against the said village of Battle Creek or the common council thereof, and all contracts

Estates, rights, &c., of village to become property of city of Battle Creek.

Saving clause.

To whom estates, rights, &c., to be delivered.

City may sue and recover.

Contracts binding.

made or agreements entered into by the corporate authorities of the said village of Battle Creek, shall be, and the same are, hereby made binding and obligatory upon the corporation hereby created.

Township of Emmett organized.

SEC. 76. That all the part of the township of Emmett lying in town two south, of range seven west, and not included in the limits of the city of Battle Creek, be and the same is hereby set off from the residue of said township, and organized into a separate township by the name of Emmett, and the first election of township officers shall [be] held at the red school house, in school district number three, in said township.

Township of Battle Creek organized.

SEC. 77. That all that part of the township of Battle Creek lying in town two south, of range eight west, and not included in the city of Battle Creek, be and the same is hereby set off from the residue of said township, and organized into a separate township by the name of Battle Creek, and the first election of township officers therein shall be held in the school house on Goguac Prairie.

Act repealed.

SEC. 78. The act of the legislature of the State of Michigan, entitled an act to incorporate the village of Battle Creek, approved April second, one thousand eight hundred and fifty; and all acts and parts of acts amending or altering said act, be and the same are hereby repealed: *Provided however*, That the repealing of said laws shall not affect any act already done, right accruing or acquired or proceeding had or commenced or tax sale made by virtue thereof, or by virtue of any by-laws or ordinance of the common council of said village, passed in conformity therewith, but the same shall remain as valid and may be proceeded in as if the said laws hereby repealed, and every of them, had remained in full force.

Proviso.

Acquired rights, &c., not affected by repeal.

SEC. 79. This act shall be deemed a public act and shall be favorably construed in all courts and places whatsoever.

SEC. 80. This act is ordered to take effect on and after the twenty-fifth day of February, eighteen hundred and fifty-nine.

Approved Febuary 3, 1859.

[No. 71.]

AN ACT to amend an act entitled, "An act to incorporate the city of Battle Creek," approved February third, eighteen hundred and fifty-nine.

SECTION 1. *The People of the State of Michigan enact:* That section seven of said act shall be so altered and amended as to read as follows:

Officers to be appointed by council.

SEC. 7. The common council shall have power to appoint an attorney for the city, one or more deputy street commissioners, and deputy marshals, a deputy recorder, who shall have no power or authority to act in the meetings of the common council, and at other times and places, only in case of the death, absence or inability of the recorder to discharge the duties of his office, and such other officers, whose election is not herein specifically provided for, as they may deem necessary to carry into effect the powers granted by this act, and to remove the same at pleasure. They shall also have power to remove the marshal or treasurer, or any constable of said city, for any violation of the provisions of this act, or of any amendment thereof, or of any by-law or ordinance, or for neglecting or refusing to perform the lawful requirements of said common council in the manner to be provided by the by-laws or ordinances of said common council; and in case of the death, resignation or removal from the city, or from the ward from which he was elected, of any officer of the corporation, the common council shall, as soon as may be, appoint an officer to fill such vacancy, for the unexpired portion of his term of office, *Provided*, Such appointment shall not extend beyond the next annual election of said city, and until his successor shall be elected and qualified, all officers so appointed shall be notified and qualified as herein directed: *Provided*, That the common council may, at any time order a special election to fill vacancies in any office which is elective under this act, in which case the common council shall designate the time and places for holding such special election, and the same notice shall be given as for an annual election, stating the office or offices to be filled, and any person so elected shall hold and serve for the remainder of the term of such office.

Council to remove officers.

Power of council to appoint in certain cases.

SEC. 2. Section forty-seven of said act shall be so amended as to read as follows:

Duties of mayor.

SEC. 47. The mayor of said city shall be the chief executive officer thereof. It shall be his duty in addition to the other requirements of this act, to see that all the officers of said city, faithfully comply with and discharge their official duties, to see that all laws pertaining to the municipal government of said city, and all ordinances and resolutions of the common council be faithfully observed and executed. He is also hereby authorized and empowered generally to administer oaths and to take affidavits, and shall from time to time recommend such measures to the common council as to him shall seem proper. The mayor of said city shall also be, *ex-officio*, a member of the board of supervisors of the county of Calhoun, and shall with the supervisors elected or appointed in and for said city, represent said city in the board of supervisors of said county, and shall possess the like powers and be chargeable with the like duties as any other of the members of said board of supervisors, and shall be entitled to the same pay and be paid in the same manner as the other members of said board, *Provided*, That he shall exercise no authority as a supervisor, except as a member of such board.

Mayor to administer oaths, &c.

Mayor member of board of supervisors.

What pay to receive.

SEC. 3. Section fifty-seven of said act shall be so altered and amended so as to read as follows:

Jury trials.

SEC. 67. In all trials before any justice of the peace under the provisions of this act of any person or persons charged with any violation of any by-law or ordinance of the common council, he or they shall be entitled to a trial by a jury of six persons, and all the proceedings for selecting and summoning such jury, and in the trial of the cause shall be in conformity, as near as may be, with the mode of proceedings in similar cases before justices of the peace, and within the same time, and in all cases the right of appeal or *certiorari* from the justice's court, to the circuit court for the county of Calhoun, shall be allowed to the parties, or any or either of them, and the same recognizance or bond shall be given as is or may be required by law in appeals or proceedings by *certiorari* from justice's courts in similar cases.

Appeals, &c., from justices' courts.

SEC. 4. This act shall take immediate effect.

CITY ORDINANCES.

ORDINANCES OF THE COMMON COUNCIL

OF THE

CITY OF BATTLE CREEK.

OF THE MEETINGS OF THE COMMON COUNCIL.

1. *Be it ordained by the Common Council of the City of Battle Creek*, That the regular meetings of the common council, shall be held at the mayor's office in said city on Monday evening of each week. Meetings of council. Where held.

2. The regular meetings of the common council shall, between the first day of May and the first day of October, be called to order at half past seven o'clock P. M., and between the first day of October and the first day of May, at seven o'clock P. M. When held.

3. Special meetings of the common council may be called at any time by the mayor or other officer acting as mayor for the time being, and due notice thereof shall be given at the request of said officer by the marshal to each member of the common council, and the object of said meeting shall be stated in the notice thereof. Special meetings, when and how called.

4. No business shall be transacted at any special meeting of the common council except such business as was stated in the notice thereof to be the object of the meeting. Business, what at special meetings.

5. No notice of the regular meetings of the common council shall be given to the members thereof, but each member thereof and all city officers required to attend the meetings of the common council, shall attend without notice. No notice of regular meeting.

The foregoing ordinances were approved on the 21st day of March, A. D. 1859, and by the unanimous vote of the common council were ordered to take effect immediately.

OF THE OFFICERS OF THE COMMON COUNCIL, AND OF THE OFFICERS OF THE CITY OF BATTLE CREEK.

Mayor's office, where held.

1. *Be it ordained by the Common Council of the City of Battle Creek*, That the office of the mayor shall, until otherwise ordered, be kept in the front room of the second story of the brick building on Jefferson Street in said city, now occupied by Messrs. M. & M. Neale, as a boot and shoe store, and that said office shall be called the mayor's office.

Recorder's office, where held.

2. The recorder shall keep his office in the room in which the mayor's office is kept, and the same shall also be called the recorder's office.

Meetings of council, where held.

3. All meetings of the common council shall be held in the mayor's office.

Offices of city officers.

4. The supervisor, marshal, treasurer and city attorney shall respectively hold their offices in the mayor's office.

Books and papers, where kept.

5. All books and papers belonging or appertaining to the office of the mayor, recorder, common council, supervisor, marshal and treasurer of the city of Battle Creek, shall be kept in the respective offices of said officers and common council.

The foregoing ordinances were approved by the common council on the 21st day of March, A. D. 1859, and by the unanimous vote of said common council were ordered to take immediate effect.

OF OFFICIAL BONDS.

Treasurer's bond.

1. *Be it ordained by the common council of the city of Battle Creek*, That the treasurer of said city within five days from the passage of this ordinance shall execute to the mayor of said city and his successors in office, a bond

Amount.

in the penal sum of twelve thousand dollars, with two good and sufficient sureties, to be approved by the mayor,

Condition.

conditioned for the faithful performance of the duties of his office and the trusts reposed in him.

Marshal's bond.

2. The marshal of said city shall within five days from the passage of this ordinance execute to the mayor of said

city and his successors in office a bond in the penal sum of eight thousand dollars, with two good and sufficient sureties to be approved by the mayor, conditioned for the faithful performance of the duties of his office and the trusts reposed in him. Amount. Condition.

3. The recorder of said city shall within five days from the passage of this ordinance execute to the mayor of said city and his successors in office, a bond in the penal sum of five hundred dollars with one good and sufficient surety, to be approved by the mayor, conditioned for the faithful performance of the duties of his office and the trusts reposed in him. Recorder's bond. Amount. Condition.

4. All deputy street commissioners to be hereafter appointed by the common council shall within five days after their appointment execute to the marshal of said city and his successors in office, a bond in such penal sums as shall be directed by the common council at the time of the appointment, with one good and sufficient surety to be approved by the mayor, conditioned for the faithful performance of the duties of their office, and the trusts reposed in them. Deputy street commissioner's bond. Condition.

5. The recorder, marshal and treasurer of the city of Battle Creek, hereafter elected or appointed, shall respectively at or before the time of taking the oath of office required of them, execute to the mayor of said city and his successors in office, a bond in the penal sum in the foregoing ordinances, respectively named for said officers, with the sureties therein required, conditioned and to be approved in like manner. Officers' bonds.

6. All official bonds shall be filed with the recorder within the time limited for executing the same, and the recorder shall forthwith make a memorandum of the same in the record book of the proceedings of the common council, which memorandum shall state the date of said bond, the maker thereof and his title of office, and the name or names of surety or sureties, and the penal amount thereof, and by whom, and the date of the approval thereof. Official bonds, when filed and how noted.

7. In case of the death or inability of the mayor from any cause to act, all official bonds shall be approved by When Recorder to approve bonds.

the recorder, except the bond of the recorder, which shall be approved by the vote of the common council at the first regular meeting thereof, after the time in which the recorder shall be required to execute the same.

Sureties to justify.

8. It shall be the duty of the mayor or other officer before approving of the sureties to official bonds, to require them severally to justify as to their and each of their responsibility on oath, and certify the fact in the bond.

The foregoing ordinances relating to official bonds were approved on the 21st day of March, and by the unanimous vote of the common council were ordered to take effect immediately.

OF ANIMALS GOING AT LARGE.

What animals not to run at large.

1. *Be it ordained by the common council of the city of Battle Creek*, That no horse, sheep or swine shall be permitted to go at large within said city.

When not to go at large.

2. After one hour after sunset and until sunrise, between the first day of April and the first day of November, and at any time either day or night between the first day of November and the first day of April, no cattle shall be permitted to go at large within said city.

Who may take up animals.

3. Any person finding any horse, cattle, sheep or swine going at large contrary to the provisions of the preceding by-laws, may take up the same, and deliver said animal or animals to the pound-master of said city.

Amount to be received for taking up, &c.

4. Any person taking up and delivering to the pound-master of said city any animal or animals going at large contrary to the provisions of this ordinance, shall be entitled to receive for each and every animal so by him taken up and delivered to said pound-master, the sum of twenty-five cents.

Penalty for illegal impounding.

5. Every person who shall knowingly and willfully take up and deliver to said pound-master any animal or animals not going at large, contrary to the provisions of this ordinance, shall be liable to a penalty of five dollars, to be sued for and collected by and on the behalf of the persons

aggrieved, for each animal so by him taken up and delivered to said pound-master.

6. It shall be the duty of the marshal whenever he shall be thereunto required by resolution of the common council, to take up and deliver unto the pound-master of said city any horse, cattle, sheep or swine going at large contrary to the provisions of this ordinance, and said marshal shall be entitled to receive for each and every animal so by him taken up and delivered to said pound-master, the sum of twenty-five cents.

Marshal, when to impound animals.

How much to receive.

7. Any person who shall willfully and maliciously enter any pound of the city of Battle Creek and take therefrom any horse, cattle, sheep or swine impounded therein, or who shall release therefrom any animal impounded therein, shall be punished by a fine not less than five dollars nor more than twenty-five dollars, or by imprisonment in the city prison or county jail not more than ten days, or by both such fine and imprisonment, in the discretion of the court.

Releasing animals impounded, fine, &c.

Approved March 28, 1859.

OF THE POUND-MASTER AND HIS DUTIES.

1. *Be it ordained by the common council of the city of Battle Creek*, That the pound-master shall have the custody of the pound of said city, and shall receive and impound therein all horses, cattle, sheep or swine taken up and delivered to him for that purpose by any person.

Pound-master's duties.

2. It shall be the duty of said pound-master immediately after receiving any of the animals so delivered to him, to enter in a book to be provided by him for that purpose, an accurate description of any animal or animals so by him received, the name of the person delivering such animal or animals, and the day of the date thereof.

Duties.

3. The pound-master shall provide necessary food and sustenance for all animals impounded in said pound.

Duties.

4. If any animal shall not be claimed and taken away by any person within forty-eight hours from the time such animal shall have been delivered to said pound-master, it

Pound-master, when to advertise animals.

shall be the duty of the pound-master to advertise such animal or animals for sale at public auction or vendue, and shall post written or printed notices of such sale, specifying the time and place of such sale, and containing an accurate description of the property to be sold, in five public places in said city, at least three days previous to such sale, and to keep a copy of said notice of sale, and of all notices of postponements thereof.

When to post notices of sales.

Where.

When to sell.

5. It shall be the duty of the pound-master to sell said property at the pound in said city, at the time specified in said notice, unless such sale shall be by him postponed, and in case a sale shall be postponed, notice thereof shall be given by attaching such notice to the original notice of sale; and in case any sale shall be postponed by him, all postponements shall not exceed five days, and such sale shall be made on the day to which such sale shall be postponed in like manner as upon the day for which such sale was first advertised to be made.

Notice of postponements.

To make return of sales.

6. The pound-master shall make due return of all sales upon the copy of the notice thereof kept by him, and within five days thereafter shall return the same to the recorder, who shall file and preserve the same.

Amount Pound-master to receive when animals are claimed.

7. The pound-master shall be entitled to receive for each animal by him impounded from the person claiming the same, the sum of fifty cents, and also a reasonable amount for the necessary food and sustenance furnished by him for each of said animals, and for advertising and selling any such animal or animals, the same fees as are by law allowed to constables for advertising and selling personal property on execution, and it shall also be his duty before delivering any animal or animals to any person claiming the same, to demand and receive from such person the sum of twenty-five cents for the use of the person who shall have taken up and delivered such animal or animals to said pound-master, and to pay over the same forthwith to the person who shall have taken up and delivered such animal or animals to said pound-master.

Duty to demand amount.

To pay over.

Amount to be retained by Pound-master.

8. After said pound-master shall have made any sale of any property impounded by him, he shall retain out of the

proceeds thereof sufficient to pay his own fees and charges for impounding, keeping and selling said property, and also the amount which the person shall be entitled to for taking up and delivering said property to said pound-master, and the balance arising on such sale, if any, shall be by him paid in to the treasurer of said city.

Balance, when paid.

9. The treasurer shall be authorized to pay over any such balance to any person who shall, within three months from the time of such sale, make proof by his own and the affidavit of one other person, to the satisfaction of the city attorney that he is entitled to the same, and such person upon presenting such affidavits and the certificate of the city attorney to the treasurer, shall be entitled to receive such balance; which affidavits and certificate shall be filed and preserved by the treasurer.

Treasurer, when to pay over surplus on sales.

10. Whenever any balance shall be paid by the pound-master to the treasurer, and three months after such sale shall have expired without any claim having been made by any person upon such balance, the same shall be and become the property of the city of Battle Creek, and shall be appropriated from time to time, whenever it shall become necessary, by the common council, for the purpose of making repairs upon the pound, and for no other purpose.

11. It shall be the duty of the pound-master at the last regular meeting of the common council, in the months of February, May, August and November, to make a report in writing, and on oath, to the common council, stating the number of animals impounded by him since his last report, the disposition made of such animals, by whom delivered to him, the amount of money by him received, from whom, and to whom paid, and the condition of the pound.

12. The pound-master shall not be either directly or indirectly interested in any sale made by him, under a penalty of ten dollars, to be sued for, and collected by, and on the behalf of, the city of Battle Creek, and to be appropriated, when collected, by the common council, to the repairing of the pound.

Approved March 28, 1859.

OF THE ILLEGAL SALE OF LIQUOR.

Duty of officers to prosecute.

1. *Be it ordained by the common council of the city of Battle Creek*, That it shall be the duty of the mayor, marshal and constables of the city of Battle Creek, whenever it shall come to the knowledge of either of said officers, that any person shall have violated any of the provisions of chapter fifty-two of the compiled laws, entitled, "Of the manufacture and sale of intoxicating drinks as a beverage," to prosecute any person or persons who shall have violated the same.

Ditto.

2. It shall be the duty of the mayor, marshal and constables of the city of Battle Creek, or either of them, whenever complaint, on oath, shall be made to either of them, by any person, that any person or persons shall have violated any of the provisions of said chapter, to prosecute such person or persons for such violation.

Selling or giving to minors, &c., how punished.

3. Any person who shall knowingly sell or give away any spirituous or fermented liquor, to any drunkard, minor, or apprentice, shall be punished by a fine of not less than ten dollars, nor more than fifty dollars, or by imprisonment in the county jail or city prison, not less than five nor more than thirty days, or by both such fine and imprisonment, in the discretion of the court.

Duty of marshal &c. finding persons intoxicated.

4. It shall be the duty of the marshal or any constable of the city of Battle Creek, whenever they, or either of them, shall find any person intoxicated in any street of said city, to apprehend such person, and confine him or her in the city prison, until he or she shall become sober.

Neglect to perform duties, how punished.

5. If any officer of whom duties are required by the provisions of this ordinance, shall neglect or refuse to perform the duties required of him, he shall be punished by a fine of ten dollars, and it shall be the duty of the city attorney to prosecute such officer.

Approved April 4, 1859, and ordered to take effect in one week.

OF GAMING.

1. *Be it ordained by the common council of the city of Battle Creek*, That if any person shall keep, or knowingly suffer to be kept in any house, building, yard, garden or field, or any dependency thereof, by him actually used or occupied, any table for the purpose of playing at billiards for hire, gain or reward, or shall for hire, gain or reward, suffer any person to resort to the same for the purpose of playing at billiards, cards or dice, or any other unlawful game, any person so offending, shall for each and every such offense forfeit a sum not exceeding one hundred dollars, or be imprisoned in the county jail or city prison, not exceeding thirty days, or be punished by both such fine and imprisonment, in the discretion of the court, and shall further recognize with sufficient sureties in such reasonable sum as the court shall direct, not exceeding five hundred dollars, for his good behaviour, and especially that he will not be guilty of any offense against the provisions of this ordinance for the term of one year then next ensuing.

Unlawful gaming, what. Billiards &c. How punished. Recognizance for good behaviour.

2. If any person shall keep, or knowingly suffer to be kept, in any house, building, yard, garden or field, or any dependency thereof, by him used, owned or occupied, any nine-pin alley, or any alley to be used in the playing of nine-pins, or any like game, whether to be played with one or more balls, or with nine or any other number of pins, for hire, gain or reward, or shall for hire gain or reward, suffer any person to resort to the same for the purpose of playing at any such game, every person so offending shall for every such offense forfeit a sum not exceeding fifty dollars, or be imprisoned in the county jail or city prison not exceeding twenty days, or be punished by both such fine and imprisonment, in the discretion of the court, and shall further recognize for his good behaviour, in like manner as is required of a person convicted of any offense mentioned in the preceding by-law.

Nine-pins, &c., unlawful gaming. How punished. Recognizance.

3. If any person shall keep in any place in said city any gaming tools, implements or materials, not heretofore in this

Unlawful keeping of gaming tools

ordinance mentioned, for the purpose of the same being used for any illegal gaming by any person, such person so offending shall be punished by a fine not exceeding twenty-five dollars, or by imprisonment in the county jail or city prison, not exceeding twenty days, or by both such fine and imprisonment, in the discretion of the court.

Persons unlawfully playing,

4. If any person shall play at billiards, cards, dice, nine-pins, or any other unlawful game, at any such table or alley, or place, kept or used as in the three last preceding by-laws mentioned, he shall forfeit a sum not less than two dollars, nor more than ten dollars, or be imprisoned in the county jail or city prison, not exceeding five days, or be punished by both such fine and imprisonment, in the discretion of the court.

How punished,

Warrant, when to issue for persons gaming, and implements, how dealt with.

5. If any person shall make oath before any justice of the peace of said city, that he suspects, or has probable cause to suspect, that any house or other building or place is unlawfully used as and for a common gaming house, or place for the purpose of gaming for money, or other property, and that divers persons resort to the same for that purpose, such justice shall, whether the names of the persons last mentioned are known to the complainant or not, issue a warrant commanding the marshal or any constable of said city, to enter into such house, building or place, and there to arrest all persons who shall be there found playing for money or other property, and also the keepers of the same, and to take into their custody all implements of gaming there found, and to bring the said persons and implements before such justice to be dealt with according to law.

Gaming tools a nuisance.

6. All billiard-tables kept or used for the purpose of hire, gain or reward, and nine-pin alleys kept or used for the purposes of hire, gain or reward, and all gaming tools, implements or materials kept or used for the purposes of gaming, contrary to law, or contrary to any ordinance of the city of Battle Creek, is hereby declared to be a nuisance, and it shall be the duty of the marshal to abate or remove the same.

Approved April 4, 1859, and ordered to take effect in one week.

OF HOUSES OF ILL-FAME AND ASSIGNATION.

1. *Be it ordained by the common council of the city of Battle Creek,* That every person who shall keep a house of ill-fame, resorted to for the purpose of prostitution or lewdness, shall be punished by a fine not less than twenty-five dollars, and not exceeding one hundred dollars, or by imprisonment in the county jail or city prison, not less than ten days and not exceeding ninety days, or by both such fine and imprisonment, in the discretion of the court. Keepers of houses of prostitution, how punished.

2. Every person who shall keep a house of assignation to be resorted to for the purpose of prostitution, shall be punished by a fine not less than twenty-five dollars and not exceeding one hundred dollars, or by imprisonment in the county jail or city prison not less than ten days and not exceeding ninety days, or by both such fine and imprisonment, in the discretion of the court. Keepers of houses of assignation, how punished.

3. If any person shall let any dwelling house, knowing that the lessee intends to use it as a place of resort for the purpose of prostitution or lewdness, or as a house of assignation, or shall knowingly permit such lessee to use the same for such purpose, he shall be punished by a fine not less than twenty-five dollars and not exceeding one hundred dollars, or by imprisonment in the county jail or city prison not less than ten days and not more than ninety days, or by both such fine and imprisonment, in the discretion of the court. Lessors of houses. How punished.

4. Every person who shall be or remain in any house of ill-fame, or house of assignation, for the purpose of prostitution, lewdness or debauchery, shall be punished by a fine not exceeding fifty dollars, or by imprisonment in the county jail or city prison not exceeding thirty days, or by both such fine and imprisonment, in the discretion of the court. Persons resorting to houses of prostitution

5. It shall be the duty of the marshal whenever it shall come to his knowledge that any house is kept as a house of ill-fame, or as a house of assignation, contrary to the provisions of this ordinance, forthwith and with or without process, to remove the keeper thereof therefrom, and Duties of marshal.

to prevent their returning thereto for such purpose, and to arrest the offenders, and to take them forthwith before any justice of the peace of said city, to be dealt with according to law, or the provisions of this ordinance, and to make a certificate of his proceedings and return the same to the recorder, to be filed and preserved by him, and such certificate shall have the same effect as evidence in all courts, as the returns of officers upon civil or criminal process.

Duties of city officers.

6. It shall be the duty of the mayor, marshal and constables of the city of Battle Creek, and of each of them, whenever it shall come to their knowledge, or to the knowledge of either of them, or whenever complaint shall be made on oath and in writing to either of them that any person shall have violated any of the provisions of this ordinance, to prosecute such offender before any justice of the peace of said city, for such violation.

Neglect of officers.

7. Whenever any officer of whom duties are required by the provisions of this ordinance shall neglect or refuse for the term of five days to discharge the duties required of him, he shall be punished by a fine of twenty-five dollars, and it shall be the duty of the city attorney to prosecute such officer for such neglect or refusal, before any justice of the peace of said city.

Approved April 11, 1859, and ordered to take effect immediately.

OF DISORDERLY HOUSES AND ASSEMBLAGES.

Disorderly assemblages.

1. *Be it ordained by the common council of the city of Battle Creek*, That whenever the marshal or any constable of said city shall hear any noisy or boisterous language or disturbance in any house, building or place, it shall be the duty of such officer to enter therein with or without permission to learn the cause of the same, and to command the person or persons causing such disturbance to cease therefrom, and to disperse from such place, and in case such person or persons should refuse to obey the com-

mand of such officer and to disperse, such officer shall forthwith arrest such person or persons, and take them before any justice of the peace of said city, to be dealt with as disorderly persons. Duties of officers.

2. Whenever complaint in writing and on oath shall be made by any person to the marshal or any constable of said city that any house, building or place is frequented by divers people who are accustomed to make such house, building or place, a place for noisy or boisterous language or disturbance, it shall be the duty of such officer forthwith to repair to such house, building or place, and arrest all persons found therein causing or making such disturbance, and to take them before any justice of the peace of said city, to be dealt with according to law, or the provisions of this ordinance. Complaint to marshal, &c. Their duty.

3. Every person who shall permit any house, building or place owned or occupied by him, to be the resort of noisy, boisterous and disorderly persons, shall be punished by a fine not exceeding twenty-five dollars. Owner of house permitting disorderly conduct. How punished.

4. Every person who shall resort to any house, building or place for the purpose of making or causing to be made, or who shall make therein, any noisy or disorderly conduct or disturbance, shall be punished by a fine not exceeding ten dollars.

5. Every assemblage of persons in any street, lane or alley of said city, or upon any side or cross-walk thereof, obstructing the free passage of persons or teams, shall be deemed, and are hereby declared to be, disorderly assemblages. What is a disorderly assembly.

6. Every assemblage of persons in any other place in said city, engaged in any noisy, boisterous or contentious language or strife, shall be deemed, and are hereby declared to be, disorderly assemblages. Ditto.

7. It shall be the duty of the marshal to prevent and disperse all disorderly assemblages of people in any street, lane or alley, or on any side or cross-walk or place in said city. Marshal to prevent same

8. It shall be the duty of every disorderly assemblage of persons to disperse whenever thereunto commanded by Duty of persons to disperse on command of marshal.

the marshal of said city, and each and every person who shall neglect or refuse so to do, when commanded by the marshal, shall be punished by a fine not exceeding five dollars.

Duty of officer to prosecute.

9. It shall be the duty of the mayor, marshal, or any constable of said city, to prosecute any person who shall violate any of the provisions of this ordinance, before any justice of the peace of said city for each violation.

Approved April 11, 1859, and ordered to take effect immediately.

OF THE PAVING OF STREETS.

Common council to authorize paving of streets

1. *Be it ordained by the common council of the city of Battle Creek*, That the common council may from time to time, by resolution authorize and direct the paving of any street or streets or parts of streets, within the limits of said city, with stone, under the direction of the marshal, or any of the deputy street commissioners of said city.

Who to make statement.

What to contain.

2. Whenever the common council shall, by resolution, authorize and direct the paving of any street or streets or part of any street or streets, the marshal of said city, or any deputy street commissioner, designated by the common council, with the assistance of a competent surveyor, to be designated by the common council, shall proceed and make out a statement in writing from actual knowledge, or survey, giving the width of the front of each parcel of land fronting on either side of such street or streets, or part of any street or streets, so authorized and directed by the common council to be paved, together with a full description of each of said parcels, and the name or names of the owner or owners, occupant or occupants, of each of said separate parcels; and also giving the width of any street, lane or alley which may be crossed by such street or streets, or part of any street or streets, to be paved, and in case the name or names of the owner or owners, occupant or occupants, of any parcel of land, as specified in this section, shall be unknown to said marshal

or deputy street commissioner (as the case may be), said officer shall state that fact in such statement so to be made by him. Such officer shall also in such statement give the number of square yards and fractions of a square yard, in front of each description of said land, from the outer edge of the side-walk, to the center of said street or streets, or part of any street or streets, and also the number of square yards and fractions of a square yard, of any street or streets, or part of any street or streets, so authorized and directed to be paved, included between the margins of said street or streets, or part of any street or streets, to be paved, and lines drawn across such street or streets, or part of any street or streets, to be paved; the outer corners of lots fronting the street or streets, or part of any street or streets, to be paved to each other, at any place where any street or streets, or part of any street or streets, to be paved, shall be crossed by any other street, lane or alley, and shall within ten days after the passage of such resolution by the common council, authorizing and directing such paving to be done, file such statement with the recorder of said city, with his certificate thereon endorsed, certifying that the same was made in accordance with the resolution of the common council of said city. Such statement shall also, at the right hand of said description of said parcels of land, contain a space for columns, in which any assessments to be made upon said parcels of land for the expenses of paving said street or streets, or part of any street or streets, may be carried out.

Statement, when filed.

3. The recorder on receiving said statement shall immediately give notice in one or more newspapers printed and published in said city, that the marshal or deputy street commissioner (as the case may be) has filed such statement in his office, and shall specify a day in said notice, not exceeding four days after the publication thereof, upon which the person or persons owning any of said parcels of land described in such statement, may come before him to correct and review any of the descriptions of land set forth in said statement; and the recorder, between

Recorder to give notice of filing of statement.

Correction of statement.

Statement, when open for inspection.

the hours of nine o'clock A. M., and five o'clock P. M., of that day, shall have such statement open to the inspection of all persons interested in such descriptions of land, and shall hear and note down any corrections claimed by such persons or their agents, and shall report the same, together with said statement, to the common council at the next regular meeting thereof. The common council may then make such correction of such statement as they shall deem just and proper, which correction shall be by the recorder entered on the journal, if any are made, and if none are made, such fact shall also be by the recorder entered on the journal, and thereupon the common council shall approve of such statement, and the said lots or parcels of land described in such statement, when corrected, if corrected, and if not corrected, then as such statement originally stood, fronting on such street or streets, or part of any street or streets, to be paved, shall be chargeable respectively, with the expense of paving said street or streets, or part of any street or streets, in front of the same, and to the center, and the paving of all crossings of streets, and in front of all lots belonging to said city, shall be chargeable to the city of Battle Creek, as hereinafter set forth.

Who to make correction.

4. The common council may, at any time within three months after a resolution shall have been passed authorizing and directing any street or streets, or part of any street or streets, to be paved, cause notice to be given by advertising the same in one or more newspapers printed and published in said city, once in each week for two successive weeks, that sealed proposals will be received for the construction of such pavement, and the furnishing of the materials, including curb stone, if any shall be required, for the same. Such notice shall state the points or *termini* between which such pavement is to be made, and that the same shall be made acccording to specifications in the hands of the recorder, which specifications shall be filed and preserved by the recorder. Such sealed proposals shall state the price per square yard for furnishing all materials and paving

Common council to cause notice to be given.

When notice to be published.

Notice, what to state.

Proposals, what to contain.

said street or streets, or part of any street or streets, in accordance with the specifications in the hands of the recorder; and shall also state the name or names of some responsible person or persons, as surety or sureties for the faithful performance of such work. Such specifications shall be furnished to the recorder at the meeting of the common council, at which he is required to publish such notice.

Common council to decide on proposals.

5. After receiving such proposals, the common council may, at its next regular meeting thereafter, proceed to determine which, if any, of such proposals it will accept, and may direct the city attorney to prepare and conclude a written contract for such paving, provided that no such contract shall be complete until signed by some person or persons to be approved by the common council as security for the faithful performance of such contract, by the person or persons contracting to construct such pavement, and upon the execution of such contract, the same shall be reported by the city attorney to the common council at its next regular meeting thereafter, and shall be subject to its approval; if disapproved, the same shall be void and of no effect; if approved by said common council, the same shall be and remain a valid and binding contract.

Contract, by whom drawn

By whom approved.

6. Upon the approval of such contract, the price therein agreed upon per square yard for furnishing materials and paving said street or streets, or part of any street or streets, shall be the expense of paving said street or streets, or part of any street or streets, in front of said parcels of land, as described in said statement as corrected, and by and in front or across any street, lane or alley, described in said statement, and to ascertain the amount of expense to be assessed upon each parcel as described in such statement, and upon the city of Battle Creek, the price per square yard as agreed upon in said contract, shall be multiplied by the number of square yards and fractions of a square yard, in front of each parcel of land, on each side of, and to the center of, said street or streets, or part of street or streets, so to be paved, and the expense so determined shall be assessed upon each parcel of

Assessment for paving.

said lands, and the expense of constructing such pavement, by, in front of or across, any street, lane or alley, which may be paved or crossed by the street or streets, or part of any street or streets, so to be paved, shall be ascertained in the same manner as in the case of paving opposite the parcels of land fronting on any street or streets, or part of any street or streets, to be paved, and the expense so ascertained and determined shall be paid by said city out of the street and bridge fund of said city.

Copy of statement.

Copy of assessment.

7. Upon making such assessment it shall be the duty of the recorder, as soon as practicable, and within ten days, to make a true copy of such statement as corrected by the common council, and to carry out upon the same, opposite and to the right hand of each separate description of land, in the space or column left for that purpose, the expense of such pavement in front of each parcel of land, as aforesaid, and also the expense of constructing the pavement by, and in front of, and across, any street, lane or alley crossed by any street or streets, or part of any street or streets, to be paved, and the lots owned by said city opposite to the descriptions charged to the city of Battle Creek, ascertained and assessed on each description as aforesaid, adding to the amount so assessed upon the several descriptions of land fronting on such street or streets, or part of any street or streets, so to be paved, two per cent. for collecting expenses, and such copy, statement or statements, thus extended, shall be the assessment roll for such pavement, and the recorder shall, within the same time, annex thereto a warrant, to be signed by the mayor and recorder, and under the seal of said city, commanding the treasurer to collect from the several persons named in said tax-roll, the several sums set opposite their respective names, and mentioned in the last or right hand column thereof, within ninety days from the date thereof, and authorizing the treasurer, in case any person shall neglect or refuse to pay such assessment, to levy the same by distress and sale of the goods and chattels of such person, and shall be then delivered to such treasurer for collection.

Copy so extended to be assessment roll.

Warrant of mayor or recorder.

8. The treasurer shall, upon receiving such tax-

roll, proceed to collect the assessments therein mentioned, in the same manner, and shall make his returns within the same time, and in the same manner, as provided by section sixty-five of the act of incorporation of the city of Battle Creek, and the same proceedings shall be thereupon taken for the collection of any such assessment which shall be returned by such treasurer as remaining unpaid, and for the expenses of sale as is provided by section sixty-seven of the act of incorporation of the city of Battle Creek; and any land sold upon any such assessment may be redeemed in the same manner and at the same rate of interest, and in the same time, as is provided by said act of incorporation in section sixty-eight, and in case of failure to redeem, the same proceedings shall be had for carrying any such sale into effect, and for making a conveyance thereof positive evidence that the lands therein described were by such conveyance conveyed in fee simple to the grantee therein named, and his heirs and assigns, and to prevent any suit of ejectment being commenced to recover the same as is provided by section sixty-nine of said act of incorporation.

Treasurer to collect the assessment.

Return sales.

Redemption

Conveyance &c. of lands sold.

Approved April 18, 1859, and ordered to take effect immediately.

OF THE CONSTRUCTION, RECONSTRUCTION AND REPAIRING OF SIDE-WALKS AND CROSS-WALKS.

1. *Be it ordained by the common council of the city of Battle Creek*, That all cross-walks shall be constructed and kept in repair by the city of Battle Creek, under the direction of the marshal or any deputy street commissioner, at such time, in such manner, at such places, and of such material, as the common council shall from time to time by resolution direct: *Provided, however*, That any citizen may construct and keep in repair any cross-walk, by the consent of the common council, and under the direction of the marshal, of such material and in such manner as the common council shall, in such consent, and by resolution direct.

Cross-walks how constructed.

Proviso.

Common council to authorize repairing.

2. The common council may from time to time, by resolution, authorize and direct that side-walks shall be constructed, reconstructed, or repaired, on either side or both sides of any street or streets, or part of any street or streets, under the direction of the marshal or any deputy street commissioner of said city.

Width of walks, thickness, &c.

3. All side-walks on Main street, between the westerly line of Division street and the bridge, across the Battle Creek, near the residence of Sands McCamly, and on Jefferson street, between Main street and the bridge, across the Battle Creek, in front of business buildings and blocks, shall be of a width of not less than eight feet, and not less than two inches in thickness, and of hard wood, and in front of other buildings and vacant lots, of a width of not less that six feet, and of either pine or hard wood, at the option of the person constructing the same, and not less than two inches in thickness, and all other side-walks on any other street or streets, or part of any street or streets, shall be not less than four feet in width, and of either pine or hard wood, and not less than on and one-half inches in thickness; the plank shall be laid across the walk, with an inclination towards the street of one fourth of an inch to the foot, and the surface of the side-walk shall, unless otherwise directed by the common council, by resolution, be on a level with the center of the street, and whenever the grade of the street shall have been established and determined, such side-walk shall be of the same grade with the street, and in case the grade of the street shall not have been established and determined, then of a grade to be established and determined by the committee on side and cross walks. Before any side-walk shall be laid, the ground shall be excavated, graded and leveled, and when the ground shall have been so excavated, graded and leveled, bed pieces of at least four by six inches shall be laid across such surface upon their widest surface, not exceeding four feet apart, and upon such bed pieces bearers of oak four inches square shall be laid lengthwise of such side-walks, upon and across which the plank shall be laid. In all side-walks exceeding six feet in width, there shall be four

Planks, how laid.

Ground to be leveled.

bearers, and in all side-walks of six feet or less, there shall be three bearers; the outside bearers shall be four inches from the ends of the plank, and the intermediate bearers shall be at equal distances from the outside bearers. No plank shall be laid less than four inches in width, nor exceeding eight inches in width. All side-walks of the thickness of two inches shall be nailed with not less than thirty-penny nails, and all of one and one-half inches in thickness, shall be nailed with not less than twenty-penny nails, and all side-walks of the width of eight feet, whenever the plank do not exceed four inches in width, shall be nailed with at least one nail to each bearer, and whenever the plank exceed four inches in width, with at least two nails to each bearer, and all other side-walks, whenever the plank do not exceed four inches in width, with at least one nail to each bearer, and whenever the plank exceed four inches in width, with at least two nails to each outer bearer, and one to each intermediate bearer. Oak, ash and tamarack are hereby defined and denominated hard wood. No plank, bearers or bed-pieces of unsound or girdled timber shall be used, and the edges of all plank shall be straight, and the edges of all side-walks shall be sawed to a straight line.

How nailed.

4. Whenever the common council shall, by resolution, authorize and direct any side-walk to be constructed, reconstructed or repaired, the marshal or any deputy street commissioner, to be designated by the common council, with the assistance of a competent surveyor, to be designated by the common council, shall proceed and make out a statement in writing, from actual knowledge, or survey, giving the width of the front of each parcel of land fronting or adjoining on the side of the street on which such side-walk is so authorized and directed to be constructed, reconstructed or repaired, together with a full description of each of said parcels, and the name or names of the owner or owners, occupant or occupants, of each of said separate parcels, and in case the name or names of the owner or owners, occupant or occupants, of any parcel of land, as spec-

Statement, how made.

What to contain.

ified in this section, shall be unknown to said marshal or deputy street commissioner (as the case may be) said officer shall state that fact in such statement, so to be made by him; and shall within ten days after the passage of such resolution by the common council, authorizing and directing such side-walk or side-walks to be constructed, reconstructed or repaired, file such statement with the recorder, with his certificate thereon endorsed, certifying that the same was made in accordance with the resolution of the common council of said city. Such statement shall also at the right hand of said descriptions of said parcels of land, contain a space for columns in which any assessments to be made upon said parcels of land for the construction, reconstruction or repairing of such side-walk or side-walks may be carried out.

When filed.

Notice of statement.

5. The recorder, on receiving said statement, shall immediately give notice in one or more newspapers printed and published in said city, that the marshal or deputy street commissioner (as the case may be) has filed such statement in his office, and shall specify a day in said notice not exceeding four days from the day of the publication thereof, upon which the persons owning any of said parcels of land described in such statement, may come before him to correct and review any of the descriptions of land set forth in said statement; and the recorder, between the hours of 9 o'clock A. M., and 5 o'clock P. M., of that day, shall have such statement open to the inspection of all persons interested in such descriptions of land, and shall here note down any corrections claimed by such person or persons or his or their agents, and shall report the same together with said statement to the common council at the next regular meeting thereof. The common council may then make such correction of such statement as it shall deem just and proper, which correction shall be by the recorder entered on the journal, if any are made, and if none are made, such fact shall also be by the recorder entered on the journal, and thereupon the common council shall approve of such statement, and the said lots or parcels of land described in such statement when corrected,

Correction of statement how made.

if corrected, and if not corrected, then as such statement originally stood, fronting or adjoining on such street or streets, or part of any street or streets, upon the side or sides of which such side-walk or side-walks are authorized and directed to be constructed, reconstructed or repaired, shall be chargeable respectively with the expense of the construction, reconstruction or repairing of such side-walk or sidewalks.

Committee to estimate expense, &c.

6. It shall be the duty of the committee on side and cross-walks, within five days after the aforesaid statement and correction (if any) shall have been approved by the common council to estimate the expense of constructing, reconstructing or repairing any such side-walk or side-walks in front of and adjoining the several parcels of land in such statement contained, and of each of them, and to report the same to the recorder, which shall be filed and preserved by him.

And to report.

7. Within five days after such statement shall have been approved by the common council, the recorder shall make a true copy thereof, as corrected by the common council, and within three days after the committee on side and cross-walks shall have reported to him the expense of constructing, reconstructing or repairing any such side-walk or side-walks, as provided in the last preceding section, the recorder shall carry out upon such statement, opposite and to the right hand of each separate description of land in the space or column left for that purpose, the expense of constructing, reconstructing or repairing any such side-walk or side-walks in front of and adjoining such parcel of land as aforesaid, as the same shall have been reported to him by said committee, adding to such amount so assessed upon the several descriptions of land fronting on such street or streets, or part of any street or streets, upon which such side-walk or side-walks are to be constructed, reconstructed or repaired, as the case may be, two per cent. for collecting expenses, and such copy statement thus extended shall be the assessment roll for the construction, reconstruction or repairing of such side-walk or side-walks, which copy statement shall

Recorder to make assessment.

Roll to be delivered to marshal.

be by him, within the time last aforesaid, delivered to the marshal.

Marshal to serve notice on persons assessed.

8. The marshal shall within six days after such assessment roll shall have been delivered to him, serve a written or printed notice upon each person against whom assessments are therein made for the construction, reconstruction or repairing of any such side-walk or side-walks, requiring such persons to construct, reconstruct or repair, as the case may be, such portion or portions of such sidewalk or side walks, in front of and adjoining the several parcels of land set opposite their names respectively, within forty days after the day upon which such assessment roll shall have been placed in his hands; which notice shall be served by delivering the same to every such person personally, or by leaving the same at the residence or place of business of any such person, if he have any in said city; and in case such person or persons shall not have any residence or place of business in said city, such notice shall be posted up in a conspicuous place in the Post Office in said city, copies of which notice shall be preserved by said marshal, upon which he shall certify the time and manner of such service, and return the same to the recorder, which copies shall be by him filed and preserved.

What notice to contain.

How served.

Return of notice.

Marshal to return assessment roll.

9. At the termination of said forty days the marshal shall return said assessment roll to the recorder, with his certificate endorsed thereon, setting forth therein the names of the persons who shall have complied with the requirements of his notice, and to what extent, and also the names of such person or persons who shall have neglected or refused for the said forty days to comply with the requirements of such notice, and the descriptions of such property, and the length of the front of each parcel thereof, as set forth in such assessment roll, in front of which such person or persons shall have neglected or refused for said forty days to construct, reconstruct or repair, as the case may be, such side-walk or side-walks, or parts thereof. At the termination of said forty days the marshal shall construct, reconstruct or repair, as the case may be, all such portions of such side-walk or side-walks as shall

What return to contain

Marshal to construct walk, when.

remain, at the termination of said forty days, and the expense thereof shall be paid out of the city expense fund by the treasurer on the proper order.

Recorder's warrant,

10. When such assessment roll shall have been returned by the marshal to the recorder, as hereinbefore provided, the recorder shall annex thereto a warrant, within five days, to be signed by the mayor and recorder, and under the seal of said city, commanding the treasurer to collect, from the several persons named in said roll, who shall have neglected or refused for said forty days to construct, reconstruct or repair, as the case may be, such portion or portions of such side-walk or side-walks, as shall have been returned by the marshal, the several sums set opposite their respective names, and mentioned in the last or right hand column thereof, within sixty days from the date thereof, and authorizing the treasurer, in case any such person shall neglect or refuse to pay such assessment, to levy the same by distress and sale of the goods and chattels of such person, and shall be then delivered to such treasurer for collection.

What to contain.

Treasurer to collect tax.

11. The treasurer shall, upon receiving such assessment roll, proceed to collect the assessments therein mentioned, against and of such persons who shall have neglected or refused as hereinbefore set forth, to construct, reconstruct or repair, as the case may be, such side-walk or side-walks, or parts thereof, in the same manner, and shall make his returns within the same time, and in the same manner, as provided by section sixty-five of the Act of Incorporation of the City of Battle Creek, and the same proceedings shall be thereupon taken for the collection of any such assessment which shall be returned by such treasurer as remaining unpaid, and for the expenses of sale, as is provided by section sixty-seven of the Act of Incorporation of the City of Battle Creek: and any land sold upon any such assessment may be redeemed in the same manner and at the same rate of interest, and in the same time, as is provided by said Act of Incorporation in section sixty-eight; and in case of failure to redeem, the same proceedings shall be had for carrying any such sale into effect,

Collection how enforced.

Land sold, how redeemed.

and for making a conveyance thereof positive evidence that the lands therein described were by such conveyance conveyed in fee simple to the grantee therein named and his heirs and assigns; and to prevent any suit of ejectment being commenced to recover the same as is provided by section sixty-nine of said Act of Incorporation.

Approved April 25, 1859, and ordered to take effect immediately.

OF THE NAMES OF THE CITY FUNDS.

Names of funds.

1. *Be it ordained by the common council of the city of Battle Creek*, That the different funds of the city shall be entitled and denominated as follows, to wit: "City Expense Fund," "Street and Bridge Fund," and "Fire-Department Fund;" and that all moneys received for fines, penalties, forfeitures and licenses, and for other miscellaneous sources, shall be paid into and constitute a part of the "City Expense Fund."

Motions to name funds.

2. All motions and resolutions passed by the common council, directing money to be paid out of the city treasury, shall designate the fund or funds upon which the order or orders for the same shall be drawn.

Orders, how drawn.

3. Orders for the payment of money by the treasurer out of the city treasury, shall be drawn and signed by the recorder, and countersigned by the mayor, and every such order shall specify the object and purpose of such payment, and the name of the particular [fund] upon which the same is drawn, which shall be by the recorder endorsed on the back thereof, which endorsement shall be signed by the recorder.

What to specify.

Orders to be entered in book.

4. The recorder shall keep a book to be entitled, "Order Record of the recorder of the city of Battle Creek," in which he shall enter the date and amount of every order drawn by him, the fund upon which the same is drawn, and the object and purpose thereof, and the name of the person in whose favor the same is drawn, in separate columns thereof.

5. All orders drawn by the recorder shall be substantially in the following form, to wit:

To the treasurer of the city of Battle Creek, Form of order.

Pay or order $\frac{}{100}$ dollars,

for out of the

Fund.

Dated at Battle Creek, 18 .

No.

Recorder.

Countersigned,

Mayor.

On which shall be endorsed the name of the fund upon which the same is drawn, signed by the recorder, as in this ordinance before provided.

Approved May 2, 1859, and ordered to take effect immediately.

OF THE LICENSING OF SHOWMEN, AUCTIONEERS, AND OTHERS.

1. *Be it ordained by the common council of the city of Battle Creek*, That it shall not be lawful for any person or persons to make or exhibit any show or shows, or to perform any play or plays, games, theatrical or other performances or exhibitions whatever, or to exhibit any natural or other curiosities, for which pay or compensation of any kind shall be required, demanded or received, without having previously been licensed to do so by the recorder of the city of Battle Creek; and any person or persons offending against the provisions of this by-law, shall be punished by a fine not exceeding one hundred dollars, or by imprisonment in the county jail or city prison not exceeding thirty days, or by both such fine and imprisonment, in the discretion of the court. License for what to be obtained. Punishment what.

2. It shall not be lawful for any person to sell at public auction or vendue any goods or other property, unless such person shall be the owner thereof, or unless such per-

Auctioneers to be licensed.

son shall sell the same by and under the authority of some court, without first having obtained license to sell the same at public auction or vendue from the recorder of said city, and any person or persons offending against the provisions of this by-law, shall be punished for each and every offense by a fine not exceeding twenty-five dollars, or by imprisonment in the county jail or city prison not exceeding ten days, or by both such fine and imprisonment, in the discretion of the court.

Not licensed, how punished.

3. It shall be the duty of all or of any person or persons who may be desirous of exhibiting any natural or other curiosities or shows, or to perform any games or theatrical exhibitions, or any other games, shows or public entertainments of whatever nature, for which money, pay or any compensation whatever shall be required or received, or to sell any goods or other property at public auction or vendue, to make application to the recorder for a license therefor; and such license may be granted to such person or persons by the recorder, whenever such person or persons shall present and deliver to the recorder the certificate of the treasurer that the amount required by the recorder in writing for such, shall have been paid by such person or persons to the treasurer of said city.

License, when granted.

Amount to be paid for license.

4. No person shall be licensed by the recorder to sell goods or other property at public auction or vendue, for a less sum than two dollars per day, or for a less sum than three dollars per month, in case such auctioneer shall desire to obtain a license from month to month; and the recorder shall not license any other person or persons, for any other purpose specified in the first or third section of this ordinance, for a less sum than one dollar per day, *Provided, however*, That the recorder shall not license any caravan for a less sum than twenty-five dollars per day, nor any circus for a less sum than fifty dollars per day, and in case of the granting of a license for any purpose mentioned in the first section of this ordinance, such license shall be granted by and with the advice and consent of any three of the aldermen of said city.

5. The marshal or any constable of said city is hereby

authorized, and it shall be his duty in any case wherein the provisions of this ordinance are violated by any person or persons, or are not complied with, forthwith to arrest any person or persons offending against the same, and bring him or them before any justice of the peace of said city, to be dealt with according to the provisions of this ordinance.

Marshal to arrest persons, when.

6. The mayor, recorder or any alderman of said city may direct the discharge from such arrest of any such person or persons upon payment by such person or persons of the amount of the license required of him or them by the recorder, together with the costs of the proceedings and the charges of the city attorney in and about such suit or proceeding; which license when so paid shall be paid by the officer receiving the same to the city treasurer.

Who may discharge from arrest.

7. The recorder shall keep a book to be entitled, "License Book of the recorder of the city of Battle Creek," in which he shall enter in separate columns the date of every license granted by him, to whom granted, for what purpose, for what length of time, and the amount charged therefor.

License book of recorder.

Approved May 2, 1859, and ordered to take effect immediately.

OF THE ATTENDANCE OF MEMBERS AND OFFICERS OF THE COMMON COUNCIL AT THE MEETINGS THEREOF.

1. *Be it ordained by the common council of the city of Battle Creek*, That every member of the common council, and all officers whose duty it is or shall be made, to attend the meetings or any meeting thereof, shall attend every regular meeting of the common council, and every special meeting of which he or they shall have due notice.

Members to attend.

2. Every person who shall violate the preceding by-law, shall be punished by a fine of fifty cents, if he shall be absent from such meetings at the call of the roll: *Provided*, He shall be present before the close thereof, and in case he shall be absent during the whole of such meeting, he shall be punished by a fine of one dollar.

Fine for non-attendance.

Fine for leaving.

3. Every member of the common council and every officer whose duty it is or shall be made to attend the meetings or any meeting thereof, who shall leave any such meeting before the close thereof, without the permission of a majority of said common council present, shall be punished by a fine of one dollar.

Fine may be excused.

4. Any member of said common council or any officer who is or shall be required to attend any meeting thereof who shall be absent from the whole or any part of any meeting thereof, may be excused from any penalty imposed by this ordinance: *Provided*, He shall make an excuse satisfactory to said common council, at the first meeting thereof thereafter, at which he shall be able to attend.

City att'y to prosecute for fines.

5. It shall be the duty of the city attorney to prosecute any person who shall violate this ordinance before any justice of the peace of said city for said penalty, in case a satisfactory excuse shall not be rendered within the time hereinbefore provided.

Approved May 9, 1859.

OF OBSTRUCTIONS IN THE BATTLE CREEK AND KALAMAZOO RIVER.

No impediments to be placed in river, &c.

1. *Be it ordained by the common council of the city of Battle Creek*, That it shall not be lawful for any person or persons to place or continue any obstruction or obstructions, impediment or impediments, to the full and free flow of the water in the Battle Creek or in the Kalamazoo River without first having obtained license so to do from the common council of said city.

Fine for placing impediments in river.

2. If any person shall place or put any obstruction or obstructions, impediment or impediments, to the full and free flow of water in the Battle Creek or Kalamazoo River, without first having obtained license so to do as hereinbefore provided, he or they shall be punished by a fine of not exceeding one hundred dollars for each and every such offense.

3. Every person or persons who shall continue any such

obstruction or obstructions, impediment or impediments, in the Battle Creek or Kalamazoo River, after he shall have been notified by the marshal to remove the same, shall be punished by a fine of ten dollars for each day during and for which he or they shall continue the same after he shall have been so notified as aforesaid.

Fine for continuing ditto.

4. The common council may at any time by resolution permit any person or persons to place or put, or continue any such obstruction or obstructions, impediment or impediments, as aforesaid, in the Battle Creek or Kalamazoo River, for such time and upon such terms as to said common council shall seem proper.

Common council may authorize same.

Approved May 9, 1859, and ordered to take effect immediately.

OF ORNAMENTAL AND SHADE TREES.

1. *Be it ordained by the common council of the city of Battle Creek*, That any person or persons owning any lot or lots or other real estate in said city, may plant out for shade or ornament, in any street lane or alley in said city, opposite such lot or lots or real estate, so owned by him or them, and adjoining thereto, one or more trees: *Provided*, That in any street, lane or alley of the width of four rods, such trees shall not be planted less than six feet nor more than eight from the margin of said street, lane or alley, and *Provided further*, That in any street, lane or alley of a less width than four rods, such trees shall not be planted less than four feet, nor more than six feet, from the margin of such street, lane or alley, as shall be directed by the committee on side and crosswalks.

Trees may be planted in streets, &c

By whom.

Proviso.

Proviso.

2. It shall be the duty of each and every person who shall plant any tree or trees for shade or ornament in any street, lane or alley in said city, to enclose the same with a good substantial box, not less than six feet in height, and not less than six inches square in the inner side thereof, and to continue such protection to such tree or trees until such

Duties of persons planting trees.

tree or trees have grown to a size to fill such box or boxes, and thereafter it shall be the duty of such person or persons to protect such tree or trees, with at least two good and substantial stakes, fastened togther at the top and bottom with strips of boards until such tree or trees shall attain the diameter of eight inches at the height of four feet above the earth.

Fine for not protecting trees.

3. Every person who shall plant any tree or trees in any street, lane or alley in said city, and shall not protect and secure the same as in this ordinance hereinbefore provided, shall be punished by a fine of one dollar for each tree by him or them so planted.

Persons planting trees, &c. exempted, &c.

4. Every person owning any lot or lots or other real estate in said city, who shall hereafter plant any tree or trees for shade or ornament, in any street, lane or alley in said city, opposite such lot or lots or real estate so owned by him or them, and adjoining thereto, and shall protect such tree or trees as hereinbefore provided, and keep the same alive for two years after the same shall have been planted, shall be by the marshal of said city exempted from one day's highway labor for each tree so by him or them planted, protected and kept alive: *Provided, however*, That no person shall in any one year be exempted for any greater number of days of highway labor than shall have been assessed to him or them for such year.

Proviso.

Marshal to protect city trees.

5. All ornamental or shade trees planted heretofore or hereafter to be planted upon or without and around and adjoining to any public grounds, the property of the city of Battle Creek, shall be by the marshal of said city boxed and protected by stakes, as in this ordinance provided for the protection of trees planted by individuals.

Person protecting trees &c., exempted.

6. Every person who shall protect by a box, in the manner hereinbefore provided, any tree or trees by him or them planted since the first day of March, 1858, for shade or ornament, in any street, lane or alley in said city, and continue such protection, and keep such tree or trees alive for two years from the time such tree or trees shall have been planted, shall be by the marshal of said city exempted from highway labor one half of a day for

each tree so by him or them planted, protected and kept alive: *Provided, however,* That no person shall in any one year be exempted for any greater number of days of highway labor than shall have been assessed to him or them for such year, and *Provided further,* That such exemption shall not extend to any person who shall have planted such tree or trees previous to the first day of March, 1858.

What exemption,

Proviso.

Proviso.

7. It shall be the duty of every person owning any lot or lots, or other real estate in said city, opposite and adjoining to which any tree or trees shall have been heretofore planted for shade or ornament, within thirty days from the time this ordinance shall take effect, to protect every such tree of a diameter of less than six inches, by such a box as is hereinbefore described, and every tree exceeding six inches and less than eight inches in diameter, at the height of four feet above the earth, by such stakes as are hereinbefore described; and every person who shall neglect or refuse so to do for said thirty days, shall be punished by a fine of one dollar for each tree that he or they shall so neglect or refuse to protect for such time.

Persons owning land to protect trees there planted.

How to protect.

8. Every person who shall hitch any horse, cattle, team or other animal to any tree planted or growing for shade or ornament in any street, lane or alley in said city, shall be punished by a fine of one dollar for each offense.

Horses, &c., not to be hitched to trees—fine.

9. If any person or persons shall injure, dig up, tear up, or otherwise destroy any tree planted or growing for shade or ornament, in any street, lane or alley of said city, or on outside of or around and adjoining to any public ground, the property of the city of Battle Creek, or any ornamental bush, shrub or plant, standing, being or growing on such public ground, the property of the city of Battle Creek, or shall injure or destroy any box or stakes about such tree or trees, such person or persons shall be punished by a fine of not less than five dollars, and not exceeding one hundred dollars, or by imprisonment in the county jail or city prison not less than five days and not exceeding ninety days, or by both such fine and imprisonment, in the discretion of the court.

Trees not to be injured.

Punishment

Trees not to be removed.

10. No person or persons shall remove any tree by him or them planted for shade or ornament in any street, lane or alley in said city, without first having obtained the consent of the common council for that purpose; and in case any person or persons shall obtain the consent of the common council to remove any tree as aforesaid, such person or persons shall not be entitled to the benefit of exemption for any tree or trees planted by him or them in the place thereof.

Complaint for violating ordinance.

To whom made.

11. Complaint may be made by any inhabitant of the city of Battle Creek, against any person or persons who shall violate any of the provisions of this ordinance, to any justice of the peace of said city, and it shall be the duty of the mayor, marshal and constables of said city, and of each of them, whenever they or either of them shall have knowledge, or whenever complaint in writing and on oath shall be made to them, or either of them by any person that any person or persons shall have violated any of the provisions of this ordinance, forthwith to prosecute such offender before any justice of the peace of said city for such violation.

Approved May 9, 1859.

AN ORDINANCE SUPPLEMENTARY TO AN ORDINANCE ENTITLED, "OF THE CONSTRUCTION, RECONSTRUCTION AND REPAIRING OF SIDE-WALKS AND CROSS-WALKS."

Pav'd streets &c. to be kept in good repair.

Notice, &c.

1. *Be it ordained by the common council of the city of Battle Creek*, That all paved streets and side-walks in said city shall be kept in good repair by the owner or occupant of the house, lot or premises adjoining or fronting on such street or side-walk, and whenever any paved street or side-walk within said city shall need repairing, it shall be the duty of the marshal to notify verbally or in writing or by a printed notice, the owner or occupant of such house, lot or other premises adjacent to or fronting on such part or parts of said street or side-walk needing

repairs, to repair the same forthwith; and if the owner or occupant of such property neglect or refuse to repair the same for the space of eight days after having been served with such notice, it shall be the duty of the marshal to enter complaint before any justice of the peace of said city against such owner or occupant, and on conviction in such justice's court, the person so neglecting or refusing to repair such street or side-walk, shall be punished by a fine of not less than five dollars, and not exceeding twenty-five dollars, in the discretion of the court, for every time he shall be so convicted.

Marshal, when to complain for non-repair.

Punishment

2. This ordinance shall not be so construed as to prevent proceedings for the construction, reconstruction or repairing of side-walks under and in accordance with the provisions of the ordinance to which this is supplementary, whether before or after a prosecution under this ordinance.

Approved May 16, 1859, and ordered to take effect immediately.

OF THE FIRE DEPARTMENT.

1. *Be it ordained by the common council of the city of Battle Creek*, That the fire department of said city shall consist of a chief engineer, an assistant chief engineer, and as many fire engine, hook and ladder and hose and bucket companies and fire wardens as the common council shall from time to time by resolution or ordinance prescribe, and of a fire board.

Fire department, of what to consist.

2. The chief engineer and assistant chief engineer shall be elected by the firemen in joint convention on the evening of the first Tuesday of February in each year, by ballot; and the polls of such election shall be opened at half-past seven o'clock, P. M., and shall close at ten o'clock, P. M., at which election the chief engineer shall preside, or in case of his absence, the assistant chief engineer, and in case of the absence of both of said officers, any fireman who shall be present, who shall be elected *viva voce;* and a secretary of such election shall be elected *viva voce*,

Chief and assistant, when elected.

Polls when opened.

Manner of conducting election.

Who eligible to office of chief. from among the firemen present, who shall record the names of all persons who shall vote at such election. No person shall be eligible to the office of chief engineer or assistant chief engineer, who shall be at the time of such election, or shall have been for one year immediately preceding such election, a member of either of the fire companies of said city, unless he shall be nominated to such office by a majority of the members of each of said companies. Officers to be approved by council. The election of such officers shall be made subject to the approval of the common council, and shall, when so elected and approved, continue in office for a term of one year, and until their successors are elected, approved and qualified. Chief and assistant to take oath. They shall take the constitutional oath of office and file the same with the recorder within five days after such approval, and the chief engineer shall also within the same time execute, Chief to give bond, &c. with one surety, to be approved by the mayor, a bond in the penal sum of five hundred dollars, conditioned for the faithful performance of the duties of his office, and the trusts reposed in him, and file the same with the recorder.

Engine, &c., companies. Of how many to consist. 3. Each fire engine and hook and ladder company shall consist of not less than thirty nor more than one hundred members, who shall be men of good moral character, shall have resided in the city at least three months, shall be over eighteen years of age, and shall be appointed members of companies by the common council upon the recommendation of the respective companies to which they shall be appointed: Proviso. *Provided always*, That whenever any such company shall not have thirty members, and shall not have been disbanded by the common council, such appointment may be made without recommendation, and, Proviso. *Provided further*, That each fireman shall within thirty days from the date of his appointment by the common council, become a member of such company, otherwise such appointment shall be null and void.

4. The fire wardens, and members of fire engine, hook and ladder and hose and bucket companies, shall constitute and be the firemen of said city.

5. Each fire engine, hook and ladder, and hose and

bucket company, shall elect annually at a time and place to be fixed by the by-laws of the respective companies from their own members, a foreman, a first assistant foreman, and a second assistant foreman, and such other officers as they may by their own rules or by-laws prescribe. Foreman &c. to be elected by company.

6. Each company may, at its annual election in each year, nominate to the common council three of its members to be appointed fire wardens of said city, for the ensuing year, and said fire wardens, together with such other fire wardens as shall be appointed by the common council, shall be and constitute a board of wardens, who shall elect one of their own number chief warden, and the fire wardens so appointed shall have all the powers and duties imposed by this ordinance, or which may hereafter be imposed by the common council. Company to nominate wardens, Chief warden.

7. The election of the chief and assistant chief engineers shall be certified to the common council by the secretary of the joint convention at which they shall be elected; and no person shall vote for or have any voice in the election of said chief or assistant chief engineer, unless said person is a fireman and member of the fire department, under the provisions of this ordinance, and in good and full standing in the company or board of which he is a member. Election to be certified.

8. There shall be in the fire department a fire board consisting of the chief engineer, foreman, first and second assistant foremen of each company. The chief engineer shall be the chairman of the fire board, and shall have a vote only in case of a tie, in which case he shall have and give the casting vote. All appeals shall be brought before the fire board from the determination of any matter by any company made under and by virtue of the by-laws, rules and regulations of such company. Such fire board shall make all proper rules and regulations for its government and proceedings, and the decision of all matters brought before the fire board by appeal, shall be final. Fire board, Chief, chairman of board Appeals to board.

9. The chief engineer and assistant chief engineer upon an alarm of fire shall immediately repair to the place where said fire is, and the assistant chief engineer shall Assistant to obey chief.

report himself to the chief engineer or other person having the command of the department for the time being, and obey his orders. Any person willfully violating the provisions of this section shall be punished by a fine not to exceed one hundred dollars, or by imprisonment in the county jail or city prison not exceeding ninety days.

Punishment for not doing same.

Chief, &c. to have control at fires.

10. The chief engineer, and in case of his absence, the assistant chief engineeer, shall have full power, control and command over all persons whatever at fires; he shall station the engines and apparatus of companies, and see to it that all persons do the duty prescribed by law and ordinance, and any person who shall disobey the lawful orders of said chief, or assistant chief engineer, obstruct hinder or resist him in the performance of the duties prescribed for him by this ordinance, shall be punished by a fine not to exceed one hundred dollars, or by imprisonment in the county jail or city prison not to exceed ninety days.

Persons present, whom to obey.

11. If any by-stander at any fire shall willfully neglect or refuse to comply with any requirement of the mayor, recorder, or any alderman, or the marshal, in aiding or assisting in extinguishing such fire, or in preventing any goods or property from being stolen or injured, or in protecting, removing or securing the same, and in case the marshal shall at any fire in any respect, neglect or refuse to obey the mayor, recorder, or any alderman, such by-stander and such marshal, and each or either of them, so neglecting or refusing shall be punished by a fine not exceeding fifty dollars, or by imprisonment in the county jail or city prison not exceeding sixty days, or by both such fine and imprisonment, in the discretion of the court.

Punishment for not obeying.

Chief to direct, &c.

12. It shall be the duty of the chief engineer to direct at all fires all such measures as he may deem most advisable for the effectual extinguishment of the said fires, and also once in every month to examine the condition of the fire engines and other apparatus together with the engine houses belonging to the city of Battle Creek, and to report the same in writing to the common council at least once in six months, accompanied by the names and num-

ber of all the members of the fire department, and the respective companies to which they belong, which shall be published by the recorder in such newspaper of said city as the common council shall direct; and whenever any of the fire engines or other apparatus shall require to be repaired, the chief engineer shall report the same to the common council; he shall also report in writing all accidents of fire that may happen in this city, with the cause thereof, as well as can be ascertained, and the number and description of the buildings destroyed or injured, together with the names of the owners or occupants, to the recorder who shall file and preserve the same.

13. It shall be the duty of the mayor, marshal, chief and assistant chief engineer, to enforce the provisions of this ordinance.

Assistant to act as chief, when.

14. In case of the sickness or absence of the chief engineer, the assistant chief engineer shall act as chief engineer, and in case neither the chief nor assistant chief are present at the fire, the mayor, if present, and if not, then any alderman present, shall designate some fireman to take his place.

Council to appoint chief when.

15. In case of the death, resignation or refusal to qualify of the chief or assistant chief engineer, the common council shall, at its first regular meeting, appoint a day and time to elect some person to fill his place.

Fire wardens to be present. Their duties.

16. It shall be the duty of the fire wardens to be present at all fires, and under the command of the chief warden, to act as a fire guard, to take charge and possession of all property removed from buildings at fires, and to deliver the same to the marshal, or, in his absence, to any constable of said city, to be delivered to the marshal to store, or otherwise protect the same, until it is claimed by the owner or owners, and upon such claim, to deliver up the same to the owner or owners, upon the payment to the marshal of all expenses necessarily and actually incurred in and about the care and protection of such property, and for which a receipt shall be given by the chief warden. And the said fire guard are hereby invested with all necessary authority for the purpose of taking

charge and possession of such property, and at every fire, every warden shall report himself to the chief warden, and be subject to his directions, and the chief warden shall report himself to the chief engineer, and be subject to his direction, and to the direction of the assistant chief engineer of the fire department; and it shall be the further duty of said fire wardens, to prevent the hose from being trodden on, and to keep all idle and suspected persons from the fire and its vicinity, and also to use all proper exertions within their power for the preservation of goods and other property endangered at fires; and all citizens are hereby enjoined and required to comply with the directions of any of said fire wardens: *Provided*, Such directions be not in opposition to the orders of the person having supreme control of said fire; and any person who shall at any fire neglect or refuse to obey the lawful orders and commands of any fire warden, shall be punished by a fine not exceeding twenty-five dollars, or by imprisonment in the county jail or city prison not exceeding ten days, or by both such fine and imprisonment, in the discretion of the court.

Duties of fire wardens.

17. It shall be the duty of the fire wardens appointed by the common council, and not upon the nomination of companies, to make examination in such wards or parts of wards in said city, and as often as shall be required by the common council, every house, store or building or place within five rods of any building, to ascertain whether such houses, stores or buildings are securely guarded and protected from fire, and whether any material or thing tending to endanger any building [which] is within five rods of any building, and to notify the owner or occupant of any such building or place, forthwith to remove any material or thing within five rods of any such building tending to endanger the same, and in case any person or persons so notified shall neglect or refuse for two days to comply with such notice of said fire wardens, such person or persons shall be punished by a fine not less than five dollars, and not exceeding twenty-five dollars, or by imprisonment in the county jail or city prison not less than three days,

and not exceeding ten days, or by both such fine and imprisonment, in the discretion of the court.

18. There shall be assigned to each fire-engine company and hook and ladder company such engines, machines and apparatus as the common council may deem necessary for the extinguishment of fires, and it shall be the duty of each of said companies, as often as any fire shall break out in said city, to repair immediately upon the alarm thereof, to their respective engines, machines or apparatus, and convey them to or near where such fire shall happen, and then, in conformity with the directions given them by the chief or assistant chief engineer, or other person acting in that capacity, shall work and manage the said engines, machines and apparatus, with implements and instruments thereto belonging, with all their skill and power; and when the fire is extinguished, shall not remove therefrom but by the direction of the chief or assistant chief engineer, or other person acting in that capacity, which direction being obtained, they shall return with their respective engines, machines and apparatus, together with the implements and instruments thereto belonging, to their several places of deposit, and as soon as may be thereafter, wash and clean [the] same; and for the more effectual keeping and preserving the fire engines from decay, the firemen, when the season of the year will permit, shall, by order of the chief engineer, at least twice in each year, draw out the fire engines, in order to wash and cleanse them, and if any fireman shall neglect or refuse to perform said duty, and if he shall willfully neglect or refuse to attend at any fire as aforesaid, or leave his engine while at any fire without permission, or not perform his duty on such occasion without reasonable excuse, he shall, on conviction, be punished by a fine not to exceed twenty-five dollars, or by imprisonment in the county jail or city prison not to exceed thirty days.

Duties of fire companies.

19. It shall be the duty of each and every person who shall be appointed a fireman of said city, within thirty days from the time of his appointment, to become a member of the company to which he shall be appointed, in such man-

Duties of members of.

ner as shall be prescribed by the by-laws, rules and regulations of such company; and it shall be the duty of the secretary of each and every company, whenever any person shall have become a member thereof, to certify such fact to the recorder of said city, and the recorder shall thereupon issue a certificate of membership to every such person, signed by the recorder and countersigned by the mayor, and under the seal of the city, and if such certificate shall not be procured within five days after the fact of his becoming a member of such company shall have been certified to the recorder as aforesaid, the appointment shall be null and void.

Members expelled, &c.

20. Whenever any company shall suspend or expel any member thereof, such suspension or expulsion shall be immediately reported by the secretary of said company to the common council; and in case of an expulsion, the certificate of membership granted by the recorder to such person shall be annulled by the common council; and whenever any fireman shall resign or remove, the secretary of the company to which he shall have belonged, shall report the same to the common council.

Secretary of company to report members.

21. It shall be the duty of the secretary of each company organized under this ordinance, or which is now organized in said city, to report on the first day of July, 1859, and annually thereafter, and oftener if required by the common council, the names and number of their members.

22. The election of any person as a member of a company which has the number of members authorized by this ordinance shall be void.

Recorder to keep fireman's record

23. It shall be the duty of the recorder to keep a book to be entitled, "Fireman's Record," and to make such entries therein in separate columns as are directed by section 1632 of the compiled laws of this State, and also to make out and deliver to any fireman entitled thereto such a certificate as is prescribed by section 1633 of said compiled laws, and to make an entry thereof in a separate column in said "Fireman's Record," opposite the name of every such person, and said recorder shall also make the

necessary entries in such book of the present members of said companies, as soon as the same are reported by the secretaries of the respective companies.

Fire buckets

24. The common council may at any time by resolution require any persons to provide themselves with fire buckets, and any person who shall neglect or refuse for ten days to comply with such requirement, after being notified by the marshal, shall be punished by a fine of five dollars.

Companies when to assemble.

25. It shall be the duty of each fire company to assemble once in each month, or as often as may be directed by the common council by resolution, for the purpose of working and examining the engines and other implements, with a view to their perfect order and repair.

Council may disband company.

26. The common council may at any time disband any fire company.

Disturbance at election.

27. No person shall make any noise or disturbance, fight, quarrel, or use any obscene, indecent, insulting or abusive language at the place and during the time the ballots are being received for chief or assistant chief engineer, or while canvassing the same. Any person violating the provisions of this by-law shall be punished by a fine not exceeding fifty dollars, or by imprisonment in the county jail or city prison not exceeding thirty days, or by both such fine and imprisonment, in the discretion of the court; and in addition to such punishment, may be dismissed or expelled as a fireman by the common council: and any person so dismissed or expelled shall not again serve or act as a member of a company, without a re-appointment by the common council in the manner prescribed by this ordinance.

Engineer's hat.

28. The chief engineer and the assistant chief engineer shall each when on duty wear a leather hat with the words, "Chief Engineer," and "Assistant Chief Engineer," printed legibly thereon respectively, and each shall carry a speaking trumpet.

Fire alarms, how rung.

29. Every person who shall be employed by the city to ring fire alarms, shall immediately on the breaking out of a fire, ring such alarm, and continue to do so during twenty minutes, unless the fire be sooner extinguished: *Provided*,

That when a chimney only shall be on fire, either by day or by night, said alarm shall not be rung, and any person who shall violate the provisions of this by-law, shall be punished by a fine not exceeding twenty dollars for each violation.

Refusal to obey orders, how punished.

30. Every person who, at a fire, shall refuse to obey any order or direction given by any person duly authorized to order or direct, or who shall resist or impede any officer or other person in the discharge of his duty, shall, in the absence of sufficient excuse, be punished by a fine not exceeding one hundred dollars, or by imprisonment in the county jail or city prison not exceeding ninety days. The chief engineer, assistant chief engineer, any fire warden, foreman, or assistant foreman of any fire company, marshal or constable of said city, may arrest any such person and detain him in custody until the fire is extinguished, when the person making the arrest shall make to the city attorney the proper complaint under this section against the person arrested.

Officers may require aid of citizens.

31. It shall be lawful for the chief engineer, assistant chief engineer, foreman, or assistant foreman of any fire engine or other fire company, or for any member of the common council, or any fire warden, the marshal, or any constable of said city, to require the aid of any citizen, inhabitant or other male person, in drawing any engine or other apparatus to the fire, or the aid of any by-stander at a fire to work any engine or apparatus at the same, and on neglect or refusal to comply with such requisition, the offender shall be punished by a fine not to exceed twenty dollars, or by imprisonment in the county jail or city prison not to exceed twenty days, or by both such fine and imprisonment, in the discretion of the court; unless some sufficient cause for such refusal and neglect is alleged at the time, and made to appear on the trial, and any such person may be arrested by any officer named in this section, and proceeded with as is provided for persons arrested under section thirty of this ordinance.

Citizens to obey.

Injury to machines &c.

32. If any person shall willfully injure in any manner any hose, fire engine or other apparatus, or mar, deface or

injure any building or structure belonging to or connected with the fire department of this city, every such offender shall for each and every such offense be punished by a fine not exceeding one hundred dollars, or by imprisonment in the county jail or city prison not exceeding ninety days, or by both such fine and imprisonment, in the discretion of the court, and shall also be liable to an action for the recovery of the damages done.

What officers to be present at fires.

33. The marshal and every constable of this city shall repair immediately on the alarm of fire to the place where the fire may be, and report himself to any member of the common council (who is hereby vested with full power in the premises,) for the preservation of the public peace, and the removal of all idle or suspected persons, or the preservation of property in the vicinity of the fire, and for the discharge of the duties prescribed for them respectively by this ordinance; and if the marshal or any constable shall neglect to comply with the provisions of this section, he shall be punished by a fine not exceeding fifty dollars.

Hook and ladder men.

34. The hook and ladder and axe-men shall under the direction of the chief engineer and two members of the common council present, or in the absence of the chief engineer, then under the direction of the assistant chief engineer and two members of the common council present, or in the absence of the chief and assistant chief engineer, then under the direction of three members of the common council, cut down and remove any building, erection or fence for the purpose of checking the progress of the fire.

Machines not to be used for private purposes.

35. If any person having charge of any engine or other fire apparatus, shall suffer or permit the same to be applied to private uses, without the consent of the mayor, chief engineer or common council, he shall be punished by a fine not exceeding one hundred dollars, or by imprisonment in the county jail or city prison not exceeding ninety days.

Machines not to be run upon sidewalks.

36. Any member of the fire department of the city of Battle Creek, or other person who is not a member of said department, who shall hereafter run, place or wheel upon

any side-walk, or aid or assist in running or placing or wheeling any fire engine, hook and ladder truck, or hose cart, upon any side-walk in said city, shall for each and every such offense be punished by a fine not exceeding five dollars; and, if a member of the fire department, by suspension or expulsion, or either, by the common council in its discretion.

False alarm of fire.

37. It shall not be lawful for any person or persons, without reasonable cause, by outcry or ringing of bells, or other fire alarm, or by proclaiming, Fire! or by any other means whatsoever, to make or circulate, or cause to be made or circulated, in any ward in said city, any false alarm of fire, and each and every person so offending shall be punished by a fine of not less than five dollars and not exceeding fifty dollars, or by imprisonment in the county jail or city prison not less than five days and not exceeding thirty days.

Age of members of company.

38. No person under the age of eighteen years shall continue or hereafter become a member of any fire engine, hose, or hook and ladder company in said city, nor shall any fire engine company organize or permit any company or companies to take charge of their hose, or draw the same to and from fires, unless the members of said hose company or companies are duly qualified firemen under the laws of the State of Michigan, and the ordinances of this city, and are members of the fire engine company, whose hose shall be so taken charge of or drawn. Any person under the age of eighteen years, who shall become or continue a member of any fire engine, hose, or hook and ladder company, shall be punished by a fine not to exceed ten dollars, or by imprisonment in the county jail or city prison not to exceed five days, for each and every occasion on which he shall parade, run to a fire, or perform any other duty with said company, and the chief engineer is hereby authorized and required to dismiss from any and every company connected with the fire department, any person acting as fireman who is under eighteen years of age.

39. No person shall sleep or remain at night in any

fire-engine house, or in any hook and ladder house in said city, unless specially designated so to do by the mayor or common council, chief engineer, or foreman of the company to which the engine or implements stored therein belong. No person shall play at cards, tipple, riot, or in any manner make any noise or disturbance in or about any such house, or hitch or leave to stand any horse, team, or other animals, to or upon or adjoining the premises upon which such building stands, or upon the side of the street next and nearest to any such building. No person shall disturb any meeting of a fire company, fire wardens, or fire board, or joint convention of fire companies, or make any engine house, or hook and ladder house, a place of resort for indecent, lascivious, immoral or illegal purposes, and any person violating the provisions of this section, shall be punished by a fine of not exceeding fifty dollars, or by imprisonment in the county jail or city prison not exceeding thirty days.

No person to sleep in engine house.

Not to play cards in engine house.

40. The present companies organized and existing in said city, are hereby continued in force, and in case the number of members of any of said companies shall exceed one hundred, it shall be the duty of each and every of such companies within two months from the time this ordinance shall take effect, to reduce the number of such members of such company to one hundred, in such manner as to such company shall seem meet and proper, and all officers now holding office in the fire department shall continue to hold their respective offices until others are elected, approved and qualified to fill their places.

Approved May 23, 1859, and ordered to take effect immediately.

OF HITCHING POSTS, RINGS AND HOOKS.

1. *Be it ordained by the common council of the city of Battle Creek,* That no person or persons or firm shall erect, make or construct, or suffer to remain in any street, lane or alley in said city, now or hereafter to be paved, any

Posts not to be placed in street unless authorized by council.

hitching post or rail, hook or ring, or other device for hitching, until authorized by the common council; and any person or persons, or firm, who shall violate the provisions of this ordinance, shall be punished by a fine of ten dollars for each violation of the same.

Posts to be placed according to council.

2. Any person or persons, or firm, may erect, make or construct and place in any paved street, lane or alley in said city, hitching posts or rails, hooks or rings, of such material, size and pattern, and at such places and distances as the common council shall by resolution direct.

Duty of Marshal.

3. It shall be the duty of the marshal to prosecute any person or persons, or firms, who shall violate the provisions of this ordinance, forthwith after such violation, and in addition thereto, to remove any hitching post or rail, or hook or ring, or other device for hitching, erected, constructed, or suffered to remain contrary to the provisions of this ordinance.

Approved June 27, 1859.

OF OFFENSES AGAINST THE PUBLIC HEALTH, DECENCY AND SAFETY.

Persons not to bathe, when and where.

1. *Be it ordained by the common council of the city of Battle Creek*, That it shall not be lawful for any person to bathe in the Battle Creek mill canal, nor in the Battle Creek, nor in the Kalamazoo river, nor in the mill pond, nor in any other water within the limits of said city, at any place where, or at any hour when, such person may be seen by people residing in the vicinity, or by persons passing or repassing on any street, lane or alley in said city; and any person offending against the provisions of this by-law shall be punished by a fine not exceeding three dollars, or by imprisonment in the city prison not exceeding three days, in the discretion of the court.

Not to expose certain animals, where.

2. It shall not be lawful for any person to make any indecent exposure of any stallion or bull or other animal, in any public place, nor within view of any dwelling house, nor in any place where the same may be seen by persons

passing or repassing on any street, lane or alley in said city; and any person who shall make any indecent exposure of any stallion or bull, or other animal, in any of the above named places, and any person aiding, abetting or assisting in any such indecent exposure, shall be punished by a fine of five dollars, or by imprisonment in the county jail or city prison not exceeding ten days, or by both such fine and imprisonment, in the discretion of the court, for each violation of this by-law. Exposure, how punished.

3. No person shall ride or drive any horse or team on any street, lane or alley in said city, at a rate exceeding eight miles an hour, and any person violating the provisions of this by-law, shall be punished by a fine not exceeding five dollars for each offense. Horses, rate to be driven.

4. No person shall throw or place any filth or rubbish in any street, lane or alley in said city, nor in any water course, either natural or artificial, and every person offending against the provisions of this by-law shall be punished by a fine not exceeding five dollars for each offense. Nuisance.

5. No person or persons shall put, place, or suffer to remain on any real estate owned or occupied by him or them, any privy, vault, filth, hog-sty, or other thing, injurious to the health or comfort of any person; and every person or persons offending against the provisions of this by-law shall be punished by a fine not exceeding ten dollars, or by imprisonment in the county jail or city prison not exceeding ten days for each day such person or persons shall neglect or refuse to abate or remove the same after he or they shall have been notified by the marshal either verbally or by a written or printed notice to abate or remove the same. Nuisance.

6. No person shall kindle any fire in any street, lane or alley in said city, without the permission of the marshal or one of the aldermen of said city, and each and every person who shall violate the provisions of this by-law, shall be punished by a fine of not less than one and not exceeding twenty-five dollars, or by imprisonment in the county jail or city prison not exceeding twenty days, or by both such fine and imprisonment, in the discretion of the court. Fires in streets.

Firearms not to be fired, where.

7. No person shall discharge any ordnance or fire-arms within ten rods of any dwelling house, unless such house is occupied by himself, nor in any street, lane or alley in said city, unless under the direction of some officer, either civil or military; and each and every person who shall offend against the provisions of this by-law shall be punished by a fine of not less than one and not exceeding five dollars for each offense.

Boys not to get on & off the cars, &c.

8. It shall not be lawful for any boy under the age of fourteen years to step, drop or jump from any train of railway cars when in motion, nor to get on to the same when in motion; and any boy under the age of fourteen years who shall violate the provisions of this by-law shall be punished by a fine of one dollar, or by imprisonment in the city prison not exceeding three days, in the discretion of the court.

Duties of Marshal.

9. It shall be the duty of the marshal and of each and every of the constables of said city, who shall be present at any violation of any of the provisions of this ordinance, forthwith to arrest any person violating the same, and to convey him before any justice of the peace of said city, to be dealt with according to law and the provisons of this ordinance; and it shall be the duty of each and every of said officers to prosecute any violation of this ordinance which may come to the knowledge of such officer, and any person feeling aggrieved may prosecute for any violation of this ordinance.

Limitations.

10. Every prosecution for any violation of this ordinance shall be commenced within ten days after such violation.

Approved July 25, 1859, and ordered to take effect immediately.

TO PUNISH DRUNKARDS.

Persons not to be drunk, where.

1. *Be it ordained by the common council of the city of Battle Creek*, That it shall not be lawful for any person to be drunk in any street, lane or alley in said city, nor

in any hotel, tavern or inn, nor in any house or place in said city kept for the purpose of public business, nor in any assemblage of people collected together in any place for any purpose; and any person offending against the provisions of this by-law shall be punished by a fine not exceeding ten dollars, or by imprisonment in the county jail or city prison not exceeding five days, or by both such fine and imprisonment, in the discretion of the court.

2. It shall be the duty of the mayor, marshal and constables of said city, and of each of them, to prosecute for any violation of this ordinance which shall come to the knowledge of them or either of them, and any citizen may likewise prosecute for any violation. Officers to prosecute.

3. All prosecutions under this ordinance shall be commenced within ten days after such violation.

Approved August 29, 1859.

AN ORDINANCE AMENDATORY OF SECTION 3, OF AN ORDINANCE ENTITLED, "OF THE ILLEGAL SALE OF LIQUOR."

1. *Be it ordained by the common council of the city of Battle Creek*, That section three of an ordinance entitled, "Of the illegal sale of liquor," be amended by inserting in the first line after the words, "who shall," the words, "by himself, his agent or servant," and by striking out after the words "who shall," the word "knowingly," so that the same shall read as follows:

SEC. 3. Any person who shall by himself, his agent or servant, sell or give away any spirituous or fermented liquor to any drunkard, minor or apprentice, shall be punished by a fine of not less than ten dollars, nor more than fifty dollars, or by imprisonment in the county jail or city prison not less than five nor more than thirty days, or by both such fine and imprisonment, in the discretion of the court. Liquor not to be sold, to whom.

Approved October 3, 1859.

OF THE ASSESSMENT AND COLLECTION OF CITY AND OTHER TAXES.

Duty of council. 1. *Be it ordained by the common council of the city of Battle Creek,* That it shall be the duty of the common council on the first Monday of November in each and every year, to determine by resolution what amount of money shall be raised by tax for the current year, and what amount of the same shall be apportioned to the several and respective funds of said city.

Duty of Recorder. 2. It shall be the duty of the recorder immediately thereafter to assess the taxes that shall have been so levied by the common council for the year, in accordance with the provisions of section sixty-four of the act of Incorporation of the city of Battle Creek, and to deliver a copy of the same to the treasurer of said city, with the proper warrant thereto annexed, on or before the fourth Monday of November of such year. Said warrant shall command the treasurer to collect from the several persons named in said roll, the several sums mentioned in the last column thereof, opposite their respective names, on or before the thirty-first day of January next thereafter.

Warrant.

Collection fees. 3. It shall be the duty of the recorder in assessing such taxes as aforesaid, to add thereto four per cent. for collecting expenses, in the manner provided in said section sixty-four, and each and every person who shall pay any tax assessed to him, to the treasurer at his office before the first day of January next after the roll shall have been placed in the hands of the treasurer for collection, shall be entitled to have three of said four per cent. deducted from the amount so added into such assessment to him.

Tax, when & where paid.

Treasurer to pay orders. 4. It shall be the duty of the treasurer to pay any orders drawn in favor of any officer of said city for services rendered by them, or for moneys expended by them in behalf of said city, out of the first moneys collected by him in the fund upon which such orders may be drawn, and he shall at any and all times receive as money, orders drawn upon any of the funds of said city, in payment of the taxes of the persons presenting the same.

5. Each and every person who shall pay to the treasurer, the State, county and school tax which may be assessed to him, or either or any part of said taxes, at the office of the treasurer before the first day of January next after the assessment roll shall have been placed in his hands by the supervisor, shall be charged by said treasurer two per cent. only as collecting expenses, and all taxes not paid before said day shall be charged by the treasurer with four per cent. collecting expenses. Deduction on collection fees, when & what.

Approved October 31, 1859, and ordered to take effect immediately.

OF RAILWAY TRAINS.

1. *Be it ordained by the common council of the city of Battle Creek*, That it shall not be lawful for any agent, engineer, conductor, or servant of any rail-road corporation, to place or suffer to remain across any street, lane or alley in said city, any train or part of any train of cars for a longer time than four minutes, and any conductor, engineer, agent or servant of any rail-road corporation, who shall offend against the provisions of this ordinance, shall be punished by a fine of not less than five dollars, and not exceeding twenty-five dollars. Cars to obstruct streets, how long.

Approved October 31, 1859, and ordered to take effect immediately.

OF VAGRANT CHILDREN.

1. *Be it ordained by the common council of the city of Battle Creek*, That it shall not be lawful for any child or children under the age of fifteen years, to idle away their time in any street, lane or alley in said city, and any child under the age of fifteen years who shall offend against the provisions of this ordinance, shall be punished by a fine not exceeding five dollars, or by imprisonment in the city prison not exceeding three days, in the discretion of the court. Child not to be in streets.

Mayor to satisfy judgment.

2. It shall be lawful for the mayor to satisfy any judgment rendered against any child under the provisions of the preceding by-law, on such child, his or her parent or guardian, giving security to the mayor satisfactory to him that such child will thereafter attend some school in said city, and will not violate the said by-law within three months.

Marshal to arrest, when.

3. It shall be the duty of the marshal to arrest any child violating the provisions of this ordinance, and forthwith to take him or her before some justice of the peace of said city, to be dealt with according to the provisions of this ordinance.

Approved October 31, 1859, and ordered to take effect in one week.

OF STREETS, SIDE AND CROSS-WALKS.

Sidewalks, how kept.

1. *Be it ordained by the common council of the city of Battle Creek,* That it shall be the duty of each and every person to keep the side-walks opposite to and adjoining any premises occupied by him or them, free from dirt, ice and snow, except such streets and parts of streets as shall be exempted therefrom by resolution of the common council, and any person or persons who shall neglect or refuse so to do shall be punished by a fine not exceeding five dollars for each offense.

Sidewalks not to be obstructed.

2. It shall not be lawful for any person or persons to place or suffer to remain in or upon any traveled street, or upon or above any side-walk, any wood, lumber, box, barrel, goods, wares, or merchandise, or any other obstruction, nor shall any person or persons hitch or suffer to stand or remain upon any side-walk or cross-walk any horse, team or other animal, or any vehicle; and any person or persons violating the provisions of this by-law shall be punished by a fine not exceeding five dollars for each offense.

Cross-walks not to be obstructed.

3. It shall be the duty of the marshal to keep the cross-walks upon the principal streets of said city clean from dirt, snow and ice, and in case he shall neglect or refuse

so to do, he shall be punished by a fine not exceeding five dollars for each offense.

Earth walks.

4. Whenever there is no plank or stone walk, a strip of land adjoining any premises of the width of which a side-walk should be constructed, shall for the purposes of this ordinance be construed to be, in all courts and places as a side-walk.

Feeding animals or teams on paved streets.

5. It shall not be lawful for any person or persons to feed any animal or team on any paved street, and any person or persons who shall offend against the provisions of this by-law, shall be punished by a fine not exceeding five dollars.

Wheeling wheelbarrows and other vehicles on sidewalks.

6. It shall not be lawful for any person to wheel, push, or draw any wheel-barrow, hand-cart, sled, or other vehicle, except baby-wagons, on any side-walk of any business street in said city, and any person violating the provisions of this by-law, shall be punished by a fine not exceeding five dollars for each offense.

Flying kites and sliding on sleds.

7. It shall not be lawful for any person to fly any kite, or slide on any sled in any of the principally traveled streets in said city; and any person violating the provisions of this by-law shall be punished by a fine not exceeding ten dollars for each offense.

Duties of mayor, marshal and constables.

8. It shall be the duty of the mayor, marshal, and constables of said city, to enforce the foregoing provisions of this ordinance.

Limitations of prosecutions.

9. Prosecutions under the foregoing provisions of this ordinance shall be commenced within fifteen days after the violation.

Of keeping side-walks clean from dirt, snow, &c.

Duty of marshal when any person neglects.

10. If any person or persons owning real estate in said city not occupied by any person, shall neglect to keep the sidewalks opposite to and adjoining said real estate clean from dirt, snow, and ice, it shall be the duty of the marshal to keep the side-walks opposite and adjoining any such real estate, as he shall be thereto directed by resolution of the common council, clean from dirt, snow, and ice, and to keep an accurate account of the expense thereof, against each separate parcel of real estate, and on the first Monday of March in each year, to file with the re-

corder a statement in writing containing a brief and accurate description of each such parcel of real estate, and opposite to each such parcel, the amount of the expense of keeping the side-walks opposite to and adjoining each such parcel, clean from dirt, snow, and ice, from and after the first Monday of March last preceding the day of filing such statement.

Recorder to file marshal's statement.

11. It shall be the duty of the recorder upon the receipt of such statement to file the same in his office, and also to record the same in a book to be kept by him for that purpose.

Recorder to make out statement for collection of such assessment.

12. It shall also be the duty of the recorder on the first Monday of April next thereafter, to make out a statement in writing containing said description of real estate, the charges set opposite each description as returned by the marshal, and also in a separate column opposite each description the interest on said amount from the first Monday of March to the first Monday of May next thereafter, together with the costs of advertising, expense of sale, and returns thereof, and conveyance, calculated upon each description, by dividing such charges by the whole number of descriptions, and to carry out the total amount in a column on the line opposite each description, and to record such statement and the notice hereinafter mentioned, in the book mentioned in the last preceding section.

Publication of such statement.

13. The recorder shall cause such statement made by him as aforesaid to be published in the city of Battle Creek, for three weeks successively next previous to the first Monday of May in each year, which shall be construed to mean three publications once a week, in one newspaper printed and published in said city; and in case there shall be no newspaper printed in such city, such statement shall be printed and published in any newspaper in said county, for the period aforesaid; and affidavit of such publication shall be made by the publisher, or his foreman, of such newspaper, and delivered to the recorder, on or before the said first Monday of May, which shall be filed by said recorder, and also be by him recorded in the book aforesaid.

Affidavit of publication.

14. The recorder shall annex to and cause to be published with said statement a notice that each parcel of land described in said statement will be sold by him at his office in the city of Battle Creek, to the highest bidder, on the first Monday of May of said year, at 1 o'clock P. M., of that day, for the payment of the charges thereon returned by the marshal, interest, cost, costs of advertising, expense of sale, and returns thereof, and conveyance. Notice of sale.

15. Said sale shall commence on the first Monday of May in each year at 1 o'clock P. M., and continue from day to day, except Sundays, until the whole shall be sold; and in case there shall be no person to bid and bidding the amount of the charges, interest, costs, and charges on any one or more of said parcels of real estate, it shall be the duty of the recorder on said sale to bid in the same for said city, at the total amount of all costs, charges, interest and expenses thereon. Time of sale. Bidding in for city.

16. The fees of the recorder upon each description of land advertised to be sold, whether sold or not, shall be twenty-five cents, and one dollar for a conveyance of each such description, and twenty-five cents for return of each such description; and the whole amount received upon any such sale shall be by the recorder paid to the city treasurer, and shall be by him retained in a separate fund until the time of redemption shall have expired. Fees of recorder on sale.

17. Any parcel of real estate sold by the recorder as aforesaid, may be redeemed by the owner thereof, at any time within six months after the first Monday of May of the year of such sale, by paying in to the recorder the amount that the same shall have been sold for, and interest thereon from the first Monday of May, and upon such redemption the recorder shall cancel such sale. Redemption from sale.

18. Whenever the time for redemption shall have expired, and any real estate so sold as aforesaid shall not have been redeemed, it shall be the duty of the mayor and recorder under the seal of said city, to make, execute and deliver to the purchaser thereof, or to his assigns or assignees, a conveyance of the same without covenants. Conveyance of premises sold.

19. Whenever the time of redemption shall have expir-

ed, it shall be the duty of the recorder to give notice in writing to the treasurer of all such parcels of real estate as shall have been redeemed from such sale; and such treasurer shall thereupon, upon demand, pay over to the owner of such real estate, any surplus that shall remain thereafter, and to place to the credit of the city expense fund, the amount and interest thereon, for which the same shall have been sold, and in case there shall be any such surplus on any such sale, and the same shall be called for by the person legally entitled thereto within six months after the time of redemption shall have expired, such surplus shall be and become the property of the city of Battle Creek, and shall by said treasurer be placed to the credit of the city expense fund.

Disposition of surplus on sale.

Approved December 19, 1859, and ordered to take effect immediately.

TO AMEND AN ORDINANCE ENTITLED, "OF THE ASSESSMENT AND COLLECTION OF CITY AND OTHER TAXES."

1. *Be it ordained by the common council of the city of Battle Creek*, That the following section to be numbered "6," be added to said ordinance, viz.:

Penalty for refusing to rec've orders or to allow deduction by treasurer.

6. In case the treasurer shall refuse to receive any order in accordance with the provisions of section 4 of said ordinance, to which this is amendatory, or shall neglect or refuse to allow the deductions to any person, provided for in either section 3 or 5 of said ordinance, such treasurer shall be punished for each such offense by a fine of ten dollars, or by imprisonment not exceeding ten days in the county jail or city prison, in the discretion of the court.

Approved February 27, 1860.

AMENDMENT TO SECTION 2 OF AN ORDINANCE ENTITLED, "OFFICIAL BONDS."

1. *Be it ordained by the common council of the city of Battle Creek*, That section 2 of an ordinance entitled,

"Official Bonds," be amended by striking out the word "eight," and by inserting in the place thereof the word "three," so that said section when and as amended shall read as follows:

2. The marshal of said city shall within five days from the passage of this ordinance, execute to the mayor of said city and his successors in office, a bond in the penal sum of three hundred dollars, with two good and sufficient sureties to be approved by the mayor, conditioned for the faithful performance of the duties of his office, and the trusts reposed in him.

Bond of marshal.

Approved on the 9th day of April, 1860, and ordered to take immediate effect.

AMENDMENT TO AN ORDINANCE ENTITLED, "OF THE ILLEGAL SALE OF LIQUOR."

1. *Be it ordained by the common council of the city of Battle Creek*, That an ordinance entitled, "Of the illegal sale of liquor," be amended by adding thereto the following sections, to be numbered, 6, 7, 8.

6. If any person shall sell or manufacture or keep for sale by himself, his clerk, agent, or servant, any spirituous or intoxicating liquors, or any mixed liquors, a part of which is spirituous or intoxicating, except such as are excepted in an act of the legislature of the State, entitled, "An Act to prevent the Manufacture and Sale of Spirituous or Intoxicating Liquors as a Beverage," approved Feb. 3d, 1855, and the amendments thereof, contrary to the provisions of said Act and the amendments thereof, such person shall for the first offense be punished by a fine of ten dollars; for the second offense by a fine of twenty-five dollars, and for the third offense by a fine of fifty dollars, or by imprisonment in the county jail or city prison for the first offense not exceeding ten days, or for the second offense not exceeding twenty days, and for the the third offense not exceeding thirty days.

Penalty for violation of liquor law.

7. No person shall be prosecuted as for a second offense, except for a violation occurring after a first conviction, and

Second and third offenses.

no person shall be prosecuted as for a third offense, except for a violation occurring after conviction shall have been had against him as for a first and second offenses. And the city attorney or other officer or person prosecuting, may prosecute any violation as for a first offense, and in all cases it shall be stated in the complaint whether the same is for a first, second, or third offenses.

Limitation of prosecutions.

8. All prosecutions under this ordinance, or under the ordinance to which this is amendatory, shall be commenced within thirty days after the offense shall have been committed.

Approved June 11, 1860, and ordered to take effect immediately.

OF THF LIMITATIONS OF PROSECUTIONS.

1. *Be it ordained by the common council of the city of Battle Creek*, That all prosecutions for the violation of any ordinance or any part thereof, shall be commenced within thirty days after the violation thereof, unless the time within which such prosecution shall be commenced shall be otherwise and particularly limited in the ordinance violated, or by other ordinance.

Limitation of prosecutions.

Approved June 11, 1860, and ordered to take effect im mediately.

AN ORDINANCE TO AMEND SECTION ONE OF AN ORDINANCE ENTITLED, "OF THE MEETINGS OF THE COMMON COUNCIL."

1. *Be it ordained by the common council of the city of Battle Creek*, That section one of an ordinance entitled, "Of the meetings of the Common Council," be amended by adding thereto the following: "Except from the first day of July to the first day of November, during which time the meetings of the common council shall be held on alternate Monday evenings, commencing with the second Monday after the last Monday of June," so that said section when amended shall read as follows:

1. *Be it ordained by the common council of the city of*

Battle Creek, That the regular meetings of the common council shall be held at the mayor's office in said city, on Monday evening of each week, except from the first day of July to the first day of November, during which time the meetings of the common council shall be held on alternate Monday evenings, commencing with the second Monday after the last Monday of June.

Time of meetings of common council.

Approved July 30, 1860, and ordered to take immediate effect and to be printed in the Battle Creek *Journal.*

FOR PROTECTION AGAINST DOGS.

1. *Be it ordained by the common council of the city of Battle Creek*, That it shall be the duty of each and every person owning or having in his or her possession any dog, to keep such dog muzzled when off the premises of such person, at such time or times as the common council shall by resolution direct; and any such person who shall neglect or refuse to comply with the requirements of such resolution shall be punished for each day he shall so neglect or refuse, by a fine not exceeding ten dollars.

Owners to muzzle dogs.

Penalty for neglect.

2. It shall be the duty of the marshal and each and every constable of said city, to kill any dog, or cause the same to be done, that shall be found off, while so off, the premises of the owner, or of the persons in whose possession he may be, without a muzzle, during any time that the common council shall by resolution, as hereinbefore provided, require dogs to be kept muzzled, and said marshal and constables, and each of them, who shall neglect or refuse to discharge the duties required of them respectively under this ordinance, shall be punished by a fine not exceeding five dollars, for each time that he shall so neglect or refuse.

Marshal and constables to kill dogs not muzzled.

Penalty for neglect by officers to kill.

Approved August 13, 1860, and ordered to take immediate effect, and to be printed in the Battle Creek *Journal.*

AN ORDINANCE TO AMEND SECTION 3 OF AN ORDINANCE ENTITLED, "OF THE ASSESSMENT AND COLLECTION OF CITY TAXES."

1. *Be it ordained by the common council of the city of Battle Creek,* That section 3 of said ordinance be amended to read as follows, to wit:

Four per cent. collection fees to be added.

3. It shall be the duty of the recorder in assessing such taxes as aforesaid to add thereto four per cent. for collecting expenses in the manner provided in said section sixty-four; and each and every person who shall pay any tax assessed to him, to the treasurer at his office before the first day of January next after the roll shall have been placed in the hands of the treasurer for collection, shall be entitled to have two of said four per cent. deducted from the amount so added into such assessment to him.

Two per cent. to be deducted.

Approved Nov. 19, 1860, and ordered to take immediate effect, and to to be published in three successive issues of the Battle Creek *Journal.*

OF MEASURING WOOD AND WEIGHING HAY.

1. *Be it ordained by the common council of the city of Battle Creek,* That no wood or hay shall be sold by the load; that it shall be the duty of every person previous to offering any load of wood for sale, to procure the same to be measured by the marshal of said city, or by some person duly deputed by him for that purpose, in writing, and that such wood shall then be sold by the cord; and that it shall be the duty of every person previous to offering any load of hay for sale, to procure the same to be weighed by some one having suitable scales for that purpose, and that such hay shall then be sold by the ton; and any person who shall violate any of the provisions of this section shall be punished by a fine not exceeding ten dollars for each offense.

Wood to be measured, and sold by the cord.

Hay to be weighed, and sold by the ton.

Penalty for violation.

Marshal to measure wood and weigh hay and give ticket.

2. It shall be the duty of the marshal to measure every load of wood intended to be offered for sale, when applied to for that purpose by the owner thereof. The marshal shall then deliver to such person a ticket stating the amount

of wood in such load so measured by him, and upon the sale of such wood or hay, the vender shall deliver such ticket to the purchaser. And any person who shall violate any of the provisions of this section, shall be punished by a fine not exceeding five dollars for each violation. Penalty.

3. It shall be the duty of the marshal to depute some suitable person, in writing under his hand, to act as inspecter of wood and hay in his absence and when unable to attend to such duties himself, and he shall discharge such duties and be subject to the same penalties as hereinbefore provided for the marshal. Deputation of inspector of wood and hay.

4. Every person bringing wood or hay into the city for sale shall stand the same in Jackson Street, and in no other Street; and any person who shall violate the provisions of this section, shall be punished by a fine not exceeding five dollars. Wood and hay stand. Penalty.

Approved December 17, 1860, and ordered to be printed in the Battle Creek *Journal.*

OF DIVISION FENCES AND FENCE-VIEWERS.

1. *Be it ordained by the common council of the city of Battle Creek*, That the committee on side and cross walks of the common council of said city, shall be fence-viewers in and for said city. Fence-viewers.

2. The respective occupants of lands enclosed with fences shall keep up and maintain partition fences between their own and the next adjoining enclosures, in equal shares, so long as both parties continue to improve or occupy the same. Occupants of adjoining lands to maintain partition fences.

3. When any controversy shall arise about the rights of respective occupants in partition fences, or their obligations to maintain the same, either party may apply to one or more of the fence-viewers of said city, two or more of whom, after notice, with or without writing, to the parties interested, shall proceed to examine the fence or fences in controversy, and may, in writing, make their award, assigning to each his share thereof, and direct the time within which Fence-viewers to settle controversies about partition fences. Award by fence-viewers.

each party shall erect or repair his share thereof, which awards shall be in writing, subject to approval by the common council, in whole or in part; and such award, when so approved or amended, shall be recorded by the recorder of said city, in a book to be provided and kept by him for that purpose.

Award to be recorded.

4. Said assignment being recorded as aforesaid, shall be binding upon the parties and upon all succeeding occupants, of the lands, and they shall thereafter be obliged to maintain their respective portions of such fences.

Assignment binding.

5. In case either party shall neglect or refuse to erect or maintain the part of any fence assigned to him as aforesaid, the same may be erected and maintained by the aggrieved party, and he shall be entitled to recover of the party neglecting or refusing, double the value thereof, in an action of assumpsit.

Penalty for neglect to maintain fence.

Approved May 13, 1861, and ordered to take effect immediately.

OF THE CITY PRISON.

1. *Be it ordained by the common council of the city of Battle Creek*, That a city prison be and is hereby established in the city of Battle Creek, and that the prison building adjoining the engine house in said city, and on the north-westerly side thereof, is hereby designated as the said city prison.

Location of city prison.

2. If any person being imprisoned in said city prison, either on civil process in favor of the mayor, recorder and aldermen of the city of Battle Creek, or on any process for the violation of the ordinances of said city, issued by any court having jurisdiction of the same, shall break said city prison and escape, or shall break the same though no escape shall actually be made, or shall by force and violence attempt to escape therefrom, he shall be punished by further imprisonment in the city prison or county jail not less than thirty days nor more than three months, or by fine not to exceed one hundred dollars, or by both such fine and imprisonment, in the discretion of the court.

Escape from city prison.

Breaking city prison.

Penalty.

3. If any person shall aid, abet, or assist, or attempt to aid, abet, or assist, any person being imprisoned in said city prison, as mentioned in the preceding section, in breaking, or in breaking and escaping, or attempting to escape by force and violence, he shall be punished by imprisonment in said city prison or county jail not less than thirty days nor more than three months, or by fine not to exceed one hundred dollars, or by both such fine and imprisonment, in the discretion of the court.

Aiding to break or escape from city prison.

Penalty.

4. If any person being imprisoned in said city prison, as mentioned in section 2 of this ordinance, shall willfully injure, or in any manner destroy property placed in said city prison, he shall be punished by a fine not less than ten dollars, nor more than fifty dollars, or imprisonment in the county jail or said city prison not less than ten days, nor more than fifty days, or by both such fine and imprisonment, in the discretion of the court.

Injuring or destroying property in city prison.

Penalty.

Approved May 13, 1861, and ordered to take effect immediately.

OF NOXIOUS WEEDS.

1. *Be it ordained by the common council of the city of Battle Creek*, That every owner or occupant of land within the city of Battle Creek, any portion of which land shall border upon any public street or lane, shall at least once in each of the months of May, June, July, August and September, in each and every year, cut down or dig up, or cause to be cut down or dug up, all thistles, burdock, or other noxious weeds, that may be standing or growing in any public street or lane adjacent to such lands, and between the traveled wagon track and the occupied portion of said lands; and any person failing to comply with the conditions of this ordinance shall be punished by a fine not to exceed ten dollars.

Destruction of noxious weeds.

Penalty for neglect.

Approved May 13, 1861, and ordered to take effect immediately.

AN ORDINANCE AMENDATORY OF SECTON 3 OF AN ORDINANCE ENTITLED, "TO PUNISH DRUNKARDS."

Limitation of prosecution.

1. *Be it ordained by the common council of the city of Battle Creek,* That section three of an ordinance entitled, "To Punish Drunkards," be amended by striking out of the second line the word "ten," after the word "within," and inserting in the place thereof the word "sixty," so that the same shall read as follows:

3. All prosecutions under this ordinance shall be commenced within sixty days after such violation.

Approved May 27, 1861, and ordered to be printed in three successive issues of the Battle Creek *Journal.*

INDEX

TO

CITY CHARTER.

INDEX TO CITY CHARTER.

INDEX

TO

CITY ORDINANCES.

INDEX TO CITY ORDINANCES.

www.ingramcontent.com/pod-product-compliance
Lightning Source LLC
LaVergne TN
LVHW021416110826
845150LV00007B/1948